The Shifting Fortunes of Wilhelm Raabe

About *Literary Criticism in Perspective*

Books in the series *Literary Criticism in Perspective* trace literary scholarship and criticism on major and neglected writers alike, or on a single major work, a group of writers, a literary school or movement. In so doing the authors — authorities on the topic in question who are also well-versed in the principles and history of literary criticism — address a readership consisting of scholars, students of literature at the graduate and undergraduate level, and the general reader. One of the primary purposes of the series is to illuminate the nature of literary criticism itself, to gauge the influence of social and historic currents on aesthetic judgments once thought objective and normative. Another purpose is to show how literary criticism has enhanced our appreciation of literary works by revealing their underlying structures and themes.

Jeffrey L. Sammons

The Shifting Fortunes of Wilhelm Raabe

A History of Criticism as a Cautionary Tale

CAMDEN HOUSE

Copyright © 1992 by
CAMDEN HOUSE, INC.

Published by Camden House, Inc.
Drawer 2025
Columbia, SC 29202 USA

Printed on acid-free paper.
Binding materials are chosen for strength and
durability.

ISBN:1-879751-08-9

Library of Congress Cataloging-in-Publication Data

Sammons, Jeffrey L.
    The shifting fortunes of Wilhelm Raabe : a history of criticism as
a cautionary tale / Jeffrey L. Sammons.
        p. cm. -- (Studies in German literature, linguistics, and
culture ; v. 69)
    Includes bibliographical references and index.
    ISBN 1-879751-08-9 :
    1. Raabe, Wilhelm Karl, 1831-1910--Criticism and interpretation.
I. Title.   II. Series.
PT2451.Z5S18 1991
833'.8--dc20
                                                          91-34090
                                                              CIP

Acknowledgments

My obligations are largely those I incurred for my monograph on Raabe: to the American Council of Learned Societies for a travel grant, to Dr. Manfred Garzmann and his associates in the Municipal Archive and Library of Braunschweig for their constant helpfulness, and to Professor Josef Daum, president of the Raabe-Gesellschaft, for allowing me access to materials in the library of the Technical University of Braunschweig. I am also indebted to Professor Hans-Jürgen Schrader, co-editor with Professor Daum of the *Jahrbuch der Raabe-Gesellschaft*, for unremittingly enthusiastic encouragement. Special thanks are due on this occasion to Jonathan Freedman, my colleague in the English Department at Yale, for advice on the Browning Society. For computer advice I am grateful to Anthony J. Niesz, associate director of the Language Laboratory at Yale, and my son Charles.

Contents

Preface

Vicissitudes in literary reputations are a common feature of our culture. They are occurring around us all the time. In some case they trace long sine waves over decades, in others they appear to occur rather abruptly. Doubtless these changes are mainly driven by the larger historical, social, and ideological dynamic. But they may also be partly internal to literary criticism, as topics appear to be at least temporarily exhausted, as excellence, brilliance, and ingenuity become abraded with relentless attention and the familiarity of what once was new. For criticism is subject to the same demands for originality as literature and art have been in Western culture since the Renaissance.

Intuitively one might suppose that a culture marked by catastrophic discontinuities, such as that of Germany, would exhibit much greater instability in literary reputations than more durable ones such as those of England or the United States. Certainly there have been great variations: nineteenth-century authors of national and, in some cases, international reputations have all but disappeared from view, while others, once marginalized if not nearly forgotten — Hölderlin, Jean Paul, Mörike — have been placed firmly in the canon. Yet, on the whole, the canon has remained remarkably stable. Despite energetic attacks on it, its fulcrum continues to be the Classical-Romantic age. As I understand it, Goethe and Schiller have been driven out of German schools, presumably by iconoclastic schoolteachers emerging from the rebellious universities of the 1960s and 1970s. This may well be a good sign, given the well known efficiency of schooling for destroying the taste for literature; the greatest prestige and widest interest in Goethe and Schiller occurred in the nineteenth century after they had been banned from the schools. But it would not be correct to draw from the pedagogical situation a conclusion concerning the culture as a whole. As we look around us, we see numerous elaborate editing and publishing projects of Goethe, Schiller, and the Romantics, some of which have been ongoing for some time, but others having been founded quite recently. The German canon is expanding, owing to the efforts of literary scholars to recall attention to marginalized or, in some cases, excised writers, but the core continues to survive.

Thus the mutability of the reputation of Wilhelm Raabe, which has developed from relative neglect through much of his career to a considerable degree of fame in the later part of it, then to idolatry in the quarter-century after his death, to disastrous complicities leading to his near disappearance from view, followed by a gradual rehabilitation leading to a position of genuine strength at the present time, may appear to be extreme in the German context. It is true that the recovery of Raabe's reputation has been a prominent, foregrounded process in contemporary literary scholarship. But, just because of its very pronounced profile, the history of Raabe criticism is significantly illustrative of the history of German culture over the last century and a half, and therefore bears implications that extend beyond the topic itself, which has, consequently, a somewhat larger extra-literary dimension than the critical history of many other writers and poets. This consideration will figure prominently in much of what follows.

It is perhaps self-evident that an account of this kind cannot be exhaustive. The secondary literature on Raabe is very large, although in the past it was much broader than it was deep. Over the past quarter century it has gradually become quite large again; now, however, the quality and variety of criticism have become incommensurably more refined. Only a detailed, focused research report could give an adequate account of contemporary Raabe studies. This cannot be attempted here. The brush will be broader, but with the consequence, I hope, that the historical contours will become legible.

All quotations from Raabe are taken from Wilhelm Raabe, *Sämtliche Werke*, ed. Karl Hoppe et al. (Göttingen: Vandenhoeck & Ruprecht, 1960-), identified by volume and page number in parentheses; supplementary volumes are designated by E (Ergänzungsband). Letters not in this edition are quoted from *"In alls gedultig": Briefe Wilhelm Raabes*, ed. Wilhelm Fehse (Berlin: Grote, 1940), abbreviated as *"In alls gedultig"* with page number.

The *Mitteilungen für die Gesellschaft der Freunde Wilhelm Raabes* (1911-43), *Der Raabefreund* (1944), and *Mitteilungen der Raabe-Gesellschafft* (1948-) are cited as *Mitt.* with volume, year, and page number.

1: Journalistic Criticism during Raabe's Career

THROUGH MOST OF HIS CAREER, Wilhelm Raabe had a generally dispiriting relationship with his public as it was represented by its agents: publishers on the one hand, and reviewers on the other (for an overview of the problem, see Heim 1953; Sammons 1987, 36-48). Since he was, on the whole, one of the more successful serious writers in nineteenth-century Germany, his recurring disappointment and persistent dissatisfaction require an explanation. Raabe had three main aspirations: to literary artistry, to a reasonably comfortable living from his writing, and to recognition as a preceptor to the nation. These purposes were not wholly compatible with one another. The more refined his artistry and originality became, the more he escaped the horizon of expectations of the general reader. Even his admirers sometimes complained that he was too strange and difficult. Generally his books did not sell well when first published. For one thing, many of them had already been published in periodicals, the novels in serialized form, a practice Raabe detested but was powerless to oppose; for another, the German reading habit was typically met by commercial lending libraries that might give a book many readers but depressed the number of copies sold; and, for a third, Germany was a poor country for most of the century while books were relatively expensive. Consequently it was unusual for serious writers to make their living from literature; most had either a profession, often in public service, or supplemented their earnings with various kinds of editorial tasks, foundation directorships, etc. From an early age Raabe arranged things so that he would not be admissible to the professions — the intelligent, imaginative boy with his outstanding learning ability for things that interested him and a stupendous memory managed not to graduate from school — and in later years he shunned every opportunity to earn money in any way other than writing fiction. Therefore, though never destitute, he had a difficult time financially until late in his life, and he continued to burden himself with financial worries well into the period of his relative prosperity.

For these difficulties he blamed the public, putting himself even further into an adversarial relationship with it, and making his ambition to guide it the more elusive. Sometimes in his exasperation he would concede that, if he could not have the large public, he would be content with his small one; he thus ran the risk of becoming, against his will, a coterie writer, a danger against which critics occasionally warned him, with prophetic insight, as we shall see. On the other hand, if he wanted his "message" to be received by the larger public, he had to be content to see it simplified and domesticated, reshaped to conform to the presuppositions of his readership rather than challenging them. Thus Raabe, who was often excessively hostile to the public, in his longing to be heard and accepted eventually became too tolerant of that part of it that was ready to acknowledge him. From beginning to end his wrestling with these problems was accompanied by a voluminous obbligato of complaint and lamentation. By nature irritable and self-willed, in coping with adversity he displayed precious little of the stoic equanimity his writings often seemed to recommend, and even less of the notorious "humor" in which his œuvre was insistently believed to be bathed.

One theme of his laments was a feeling of being ignored and neglected, and of ill will on the part of the critics. This was not exactly true. Most of his book publications were evaluated by critics, and the response was more mixed than consistently negative. One scholar collected 146 reviews from Germany, Austria, and Switzerland, containing not a single total rejection (Roloff [Sen.] 1953). What really dismayed Raabe was that the reviews, even when enthusiastic, never led to substantial sales of his books upon publication, and his bitterness at this form of neglect lasted well into the epoch when his popularity began to rise significantly and sales of his earlier works escalated. He tended, probably willfully, to confuse the two kinds of reception. For example, *Horacker* in 1876 received mostly very good reviews, but since they did not spur sales, he asserted that the novel had been "totgeschwiegen" (12: 545). However, when reviewing the critical record, one might sympathize with his feeling of isolation, even when he was the object of prolix discussion, for, except for an occasional flash of insight, an uncharacteristically thoughtful reflection, often by a fellow writer, or an intermittent well-turned phrase, the journalistic criticism that accompanied his career was uniformly mediocre.

This was generally true of post-Romantic literary criticism in nineteenth-century Germany. There are few critics of the stature of the outstanding ones in England and France at the time, and it would not be much of an exaggeration to say that there is no criticism of Raabe contemporary with him that one would want to read for any reason other than as an exercise in reception history. "Literary criticism" has never meant in German what it has come to mean in English usage: the whole spectrum of aesthetic, intellectual and scholarly evaluation and interpretation of literature. *Literaturkritik* has always denoted a form of journalism, with all the connotations of shallowness, impermanence, and perhaps meretriciousness implied by that genre, especially in the European context, and it has been felt to be distinct from what came to be called *Literaturwissenschaft*, the scholarly study of literature (Hohendahl 1988, 1-2). However, this is not the whole story. Among the critics there are men (women were vanishingly rare) of intelligence and some standing in the intellectual community, yet in most cases they did not do much to lift the level of discourse. It was a criticism carried on not so much in a spirit of inquiry as of adjudication according to predefined norms:

> Criticism assumes the task of regulating literature both in its production and in its reception. Thus the treatment in reviews always involves a decision as to whether an individual work should be accepted within the canon of literature or excluded from it. (269)

In Raabe's case its most striking feature is its static character. His career may be said to have run, as far as the public was concerned, from 1856, when his first work, *Die Chronik der Sperlingsgasse*, appeared, to the posthumous publication in 1911 of the fragmentary novel *Altershausen*. These fifty-six years saw his writing undergo a substantial evolution, and they were, of course, years of great historical and social change, encompassing the accelerating industrialization of Germany with its attendant class stresses, the unification of the nation, and its transformation from a backwater of parochial states into a European power, all matters reflected in one way or another in his fiction. Yet the terms of the discourse about him remained maddeningly the same, as though it were in some charmed way out of time, and this, in fact, may have led to an ultimately near-fatal misperception that Raabe himself was somehow out of time. Sometimes one wonders whether the critics over the years had been reading only the criticism, not the texts. But this was not peculiar to Raabe; Hohendahl has observed that generally in German criticism "the theoretical system is more important than the individual text" (269), and he adds:

> The industrial revolution that begins in the 1850s changes within a generation the structure of German society and thus the composition of the reading public, but the institution of criticism at first hardly participates in this structural change. (272)

One of the most familiar examples of the recurrence of critical leitmotifs over decades is the association of Raabe's style and form with those of Jean Paul. Although Raabe in an early interview (1861) remarked that he had read less of Jean Paul than one might think (E 2: 68), he alludes to his predecessor here and there, and there is a sense in which his type of fiction lies in a tradition that includes Jean Paul and, before him, Henry Fielding and Laurence Sterne, both more important for the novel in Germany than in their own country. But the critics are not so much concerned with the definition of this heritage and its relative weight than with pigeon-holing Raabe with what comes to be a code word. Raabe's very first reviewer, Ludwig Rellstab on the *Chronik*, made the connection, though cautiously:

> Der Dichter hat eine angesehene Verwandtschaft, z. B. mit dem dänischen Andersen, ja in einem entfernten Grade mit einem der höchsten Verwandten, den es in der Literatenfamilie gibt, mit Jean Paul. Bei alledem hat er vollständig sein eigenes Haus und Hof und lebt nicht von seinen Verwandten. (1: 432)

This positive and somewhat qualified association with Jean Paul appears from time to time, for example in 1881 in a review of *Das Horn von Wanza*, in which it is remarked that Raabe possesses "ein gut Teil dessen, was wir an Jean Paul bewundern" (14: 492). The Naturalist Hermann Conradi, in his overall praise of Raabe — there will be more to say about this phenomenon farther along — compared his style in 1886 with that of Jean Paul (16: 549). Raabe's friend Wilhelm Jensen, in an 1879 review of the novella collection, *Krähenfelder Geschichten*, opposed Raabe's artistic economy to Jean Paul's formlessness (11: 476), and an anonymous reviewer of *Pfisters Mühle* and *Villa Schönow* in 1886 followed him in this judgment. Otto Preuss, in a review of the second edition of *Die Leute aus dem Walde* in 1890, characterized Raabe's tone as a "Mischung von zahmem Jean Paul und zahmem E. T. A. Hoffmann," adding that Raabe was less disorderly than Jean Paul, more moderate in characterization than Hoffmann, and superior to both in "Gemütswahrheit und Gedankentiefe" (5: 454). In a somewhat ambiguous review of the same work Raabe is even said to be what Jean Paul was alleged to have been (5: 454-55). At other times the comparison was made at Raabe's expense. A reviewer of *Die Kinder von Finkenrode* in 1859 found that Raabe lacked Jean Paul's "große, weittragende Gedankenflüge und leuchtende Geistesblitze" (2: 527).

However, this was not the main line of the trope, which was rather to identify Jean Paul as a distinctly negative model. This, too, begins early. Two reviewers of *Die Kinder von Finkenrode* in 1859 complained of a dependence on Jean Paul, one of "jenen sentimentalen, bilderhaschenden, träumerischen Witz eines Jean Paul, der die rasche Entwicklung der Handlung nur hemmt"; the other that the characters fall "ins Carikirte und Fratzenhafte" (2: 529-30). Both advise Raabe to outgrow his alleged dependence. Sometimes reviewers praised him *despite* his "jeanpaulisierende[ ] Manier," as did both Robert Prutz in a positive review of *Die Leute aus dem Walde* in 1863 (5: 448) and an anonymous in a notice of *Der Schüdderump* in 1870 (8: 405). But just as often the comparison was purely negative. In 1865 Rudolf Gottschall rejected the trio of narrators in *Drei Federn* as "jeanpaulisierende Methode" (9/1: 493); in 1892 a reviewer misinterpreted Raabe's mild spoof of the critics' obsession with Jean Paul in *Gutmanns Reisen,* claiming instead that Jean Paul's influence had compromised Raabe's independence (18: 477). Right-wing criticism, which was generally hostile to Raabe because of his indifference to Christianity, sometimes took a

similar tack. The *Kreuzzeitung,* commenting on *Gutmanns Reisen,* observed that only the existence of a coterie of admirers could
explain how it ever got published, and excoriated its "silben-
stechende[r] Wortwitzelei und Jean Paul'sche[r] Geistesschwel-
gerei" (quoted by Raabe in a letter, 18: 471), and in 1895 the
Allgemeine konservative Monatsschrift complained yet again of
"Jean Paulsche Manier" in the *second* edition of *Drei Federn* (9/1:
494). In 1895 Jean Paul had been dead for seventy years, yet he
continued to bedevil the relationship between Raabe and his critics.
Nor was this the end of it. In 1960, Rudolf Majut, in his account of
the nineteenth-century novel in *Deutsche Philologie im Aufriß,*
attacked Raabe as a pretentious, less than mediocre, trivial,
repetitive, and undisciplined writer: "der schlimmste Manierist
seit Jean Paul" (Majut 1960, 2: cols. 1511-12).

It would seem plausible that poor "Jean Paul" is being employed
here as a shorthand for something more elaborate. The reiterated
critique of the two editions of *Drei Federn* thirty years apart
indicates what that was. Significantly, it was just that aspect of
Raabe's fiction that has contributed to his increased standing today:
his ingenious experimentation with narrative perspective. "Jean
Paul" stood for disorder, subjectivity, authorial self-indulgence and
intrusiveness, a form of narration calling attention to itself instead
of being transparent to the narrated. "Jean Paul" stood for the
Romantic and the old-fashioned. What we see as proto-modern in
Raabe was seen in his time as an atavistic throwback to a surpassed
mode, a circumstance that throws an interesting light on the neo-
Romantic component of modernism. It was one of Raabe's major
conflicts with his public that he ran squarely into a dogma of
"objective narration," of a "programmatic realism" unmediated by
the audible presence of an author, that preoccupied German
theoreticians of fiction beginning at mid-century (see Hellmann
1968, 165-217, and Steinecke 1975, 1: 201-31). The conflicting triple
narrative perspective of *Drei Federn* has no counterpart in Jean
Paul per se; it was doing *anything* with narrative perspective that
was found unacceptable, old-fashioned, and thus Jean-Paulian.
This can be seen clearly in Julian Schmidt's accusation that Karl
Gutzkow's experimental "Roman des Nebeneinander," *Die Ritter
vom Geiste* (1850-51), belonged to the tradition of Jean Paul
(Hohendahl 1988, 266), though today's reader would have a difficult
time associating Gutzkow's attempt to sink a shaft through the

simultaneous layers of society with any work of the older writer. As far as I am familiar with the record, no critic for more than half a century asked what it might be that Raabe was trying to do with narration. Everyone agreed that he should not be doing it; the difference was that some thought his "mannerisms" devalued his work, while others appreciated all the same the message that could be abstracted despite the deplorable form.

These objections can be found throughout his career, though they increase in frequency and irritability as he begins, from our point of view, to hit his stride as a major writer. A reviewer of *Meister Autor* complained in 1875 of too many narrative reflections: "wer eine gut angelegte, klar und ruhig ausgeführte Erzählung sucht, dürfte hier wenig befriedigt werden" (11: 455). *Meister Autor*, of course, is a first-person narration told by a narrator of questionable character. Whether a work was narrated in the first or the third person seems to have made no difference to the critics; nowhere, as far as I can see, is there any sensitivity to Raabe's experimentation with narrative voices and the spaces between them. In 1880 the Swiss critic J. J. Honegger was exasperated by *Deutscher Adel*, complaining of too little plot and too much authorial intervention, and confessing that he just could not figure it out (13: 440-41). It seems to me that anyone who cannot follow *Deutscher Adel* is not trying. In the same year there appeared what Raabe called a "dumme Besprechung" of *Alte Nester* in the renowned *Neue Freie Presse* of Vienna, which denounced the novel for boring mannerisms. This review Raabe kept in his wallet for eleven years, "zum Trost," as he claimed (14: 460). In 1883 *Prinzessin Fisch* drew a quite divided response, much of which turned on matters of narration. Paul Schlenther observed that the soul of the story was more beautiful and stronger than its body, by which he meant that the narration lacked objectivity; he also complained of the leitmotifs attached to figures, a device by which Raabe seems to us so obviously to prefigure Thomas Mann. Schlenther also remarked that the story had been published in a journal edited by Friedrich Spielhagen, even though it violated his well-known theoretical insistence on objective narration. Schlenther does not seem to have drawn the further conclusion that perhaps Spielhagen himself was less dogmatic than his theory of the novel was taken to be (15: 628). Another reviewer of the same work,

Hellmuth Mielke, found his admiration of the content spoiled by the form; he was offended that Raabe made his characters reflect on the events instead of reciting them in a straightforward way in his own voice, and proclaimed that even humor must subordinate itself to the alleged laws of the art of the novel: "d. h. der Epiker muß *objektiviren*,muß uns die Dinge zeigen ... so, daß wir sie als Objekte der Wirklichkeit, nicht als subjektive Träumereien auffassen," and consequently Raabe had not advanced the German novel since *Der Hungerpastor* (15: 629-30) — an observation that is just enough, but more the fault of the literary environment than of Raabe. One Paul von Szczepanski in 1891 found *Stopfkuchen* unpalatable because Raabe did not highlight the murder story and made it so difficult to extract it from Stopfkuchen, and he dismissed the narrative frame as superfluous. To this refusal of perception Raabe could only react with despairing irony (18: 434). A reviewer of *Hastenbeck* in 1898 once more objected to authorial intrusion, Raabe's old bad habit (20: 429). Another belonged to those who argued for an appreciation of Raabe's "Herzenswärme, Glaubensstärke und Lauterkeit der Gesinnung" despite the subjective, intrusive authorial manner that will put many readers off (20: 431). Four years earlier, Ferdinand Avenarius in *Der Kunstwart* had remarked of the opening of *Kloster Lugau*: "bis hart an die Grenze des Erträglichen geht das Heckenbuschartige der Komposition am Anfange der Geschichte beinah mir selber" (19: 418). By 1894 we are well within the period of modernism and *Der Kunstwart* was on the front line of the new aesthetic sensibility; nevertheless a cosmopolitan critic like Avenarius has difficulty coping with a novel that deviates from four-square, straight-line, "objective" narration.

Another of the enduring shibboleths of the critics was "humor." German *Humor* has a meaning rather different from that of the corresponding word in English. It is an idealistic term, connoting a balanced equanimity poised above the conflicts and troubles of common life, generally implying a transcendental, harmonious unity of all things. It does not necessarily subsume the comic or the amusing, but is a benignly smiling faculty. Raabe often applied the term to himself and his characters; some of his works, notably *Horacker*, seem like illustrations of the German meaning of humor. Among the critics, however, the term rapidly became a cliché, a substitute for thought and differentiation. It may well have been this endless, empty repetition that caused Raabe in time to distance himself from the term. In 1877, in reply to a request for a contribution to an anthology of humor, he remarked: "Was der Deutsche 'Humor' nennt, ist oft ganz und gar das Gegentheil desselben" (E 2: 193). By 1885 he had become edgier:

> Aber leider muß ich Ihnen gestehen, daß ich an den Erfolg Ihres Unternehmens, so zu sagen an die Berechtigung eines "humoristischen Deutschlands" nicht recht glauben kann. Wir armen Narren fallen da immer von Neuem auf die alte Redensart von dem Berufe des deutschen Volks zum Humor hinein! Ich für mein Theil habe während meiner Zeit nur sehr wenig von dieser Auserwählung unserer Nation vor anderen in die Erfahrung bekommen, und in diesem laufenden Jahr, in welchem der Verleger die Auflage meines "Dräumlings" zu einer Mark das Exemplar losschlägt, weil er es für einen Thaler nicht losgeworden ist, tanze ich nicht mit, um diesem Volk "Spaß" zu machen. (E 2: 245)

His biographer H. A. Krüger reports him as saying more than once: "Was die Leute nur wollen, ich bin weit mehr Tragiker als Humorist" (E 4: 306). From the point of view of the modern interpreter the problem is that the cliché masks not so much Raabe's tragic as his comic and satirical aspect.

The discourse about humor sets in promptly in Raabe's career. The prominent and able critic Levin Schücking, in a review of *Ein Frühling* in 1858, speaks of Raabe's humoristic gift and compares him in this regard to Dickens, though not quite favorably, for he finds him lacking in Dickens's virtuosity of characterization, more harmless, even childish. Two years later Hermann Marggraf, commenting on the same novel, found that humor penetrated "den ganzen Körper der Erzählung" (1: 480). The mixed reviews of *Die Kinder von Finkenrode* in 1859 repeatedly found occasion to praise at least the quality of humor, though again Raabe was compared unfavorably to Dickens (2: 526-29, esp. 528). Rudolf Sonnenburg in his review of *Die Leute aus dem Walde* is again reminded of the contemporary English novel, though in Raabe's case he finds the humor sometimes forced (5: 449). By 1881 this judgment had become reversed: a reviewer of *Das Horn von*

Wanza found that Germans are wrong to think that they have no Dickens, whom Raabe resembles in several ways, among them healthy humor (14: 492). This is the first indication that, in an epoch that returned again and again to Dickens and Thackeray in its search for models for the German novel (Hohendahl 1988, 266), one critic recognized that Raabe had actually assimilated to advantage what had been theoretically demanded. In 1864, on the occasion of the third edition of the *Chronik*, a reviewer finds an alternation of "Darstellungen eines sprudelnden kecken Humors [mit] der naiven Innigkeit," and considers that the book could only have been written "von einem gemüthvollen Deutschen" (1: 438). Upon the fourth edition in 1866, Raabe's humor, which extends unbroken through *Der Hungerpastor* and *Drei Federn*, is said to be valuable in times of political uncertainty (1: 439). In 1870 Honegger fulsomely praised the quality of humor in *Der Schüdderump* (8:404-05). Since this is the darkest, most bleakly pessimistic of all of Raabe's major novels, one must conclude either that Honegger, a regular reviewer of Raabe's works, could not read, or that the term has acquired an elasticity that begins to escape definition. The latter likelihood is reinforced by Honegger's praise, two years later, of true humor in *Der Dräumling*, one of the most uproariously comic of Raabe's works (10: 463). One could go on endlessly in this vein, but a couple of further citations shed some light on why humor was such an obsession: a reviewer of *Fabian und Sebastian* in 1882 called attention to the amelioration of tragedy by humor, the "Verbindung von Idealismus und Realismus" (15: 578). Eight years later a reviewer of the second edition of *Die Leute aus dem Walde* praised Raabe as a true realist because his representation of the world included "ideale[ ] Stimmungen," as opposed to "Schmutz-realismus" (5: 454). In the following year Raabe's friend Edmund Sträter asserted apropos of *Stopfkuchen* that Raabe had solved the riddle of life as a humorist, defined as an idealist and realist in one person (18: 431; Raabe, pleased as always to be received positively, nevertheless hinted in his letter of thanks that Sträter had not entirely understood the novel [431-32]).

The maintenance of an idealistic, transcendental dimension in realism was an obsession of the theoreticians and critics of this period. True realism, they insisted, transfigures reality (Hohendahl 1988, 260-61). Increasingly this concept of true realism, open to the superintending ethical connection of things, came to oppose itself to the gritty, numbly mimetic reproduction of reality by Naturalism. Hohendahl's observation that "even the programmatic German realists rigidly condemn as 'naturalism' the materialist realisms they observe, for example and above all, in France" (258) can be nowhere more clearly exemplified than in the Raabe criticism. In the 1880s and 1890s he is increasingly seen as a kind of talisman employed against the threat of Naturalism. The important critic Fritz Mauthner, commenting on *Stopfkuchen* in 1891 (rather coolly, incidentally, on account of its "Jean-Paulian" form), recommended that the Naturalists should study Raabe, for he has what Ibsen does not: smiling humor (18: 432). The equally prominent Avenarius in 1894 praised the milieu descriptions in *Kloster Lugau* as non-Naturalistic, not constructed according to a formula like Zola's (19: 419). In 1898 a commentator on the second edition of *Der Schüdderump* sets its poetic realism against Naturalism, remarking that Raabe did not turn poor people into animals like Gerhart Hauptmann, then going on to say: "ja über all diesem Armeleuteelend strahlt noch der Bogen eines göttlichen Humors," and expressing the hope that such a book might be a way "zu dem Ziele einer harmonischen Ausgleichung der zur Zeit so schroff bestehenden sozialen Gegensätze" (8: 408). Once again humor is found where one would least expect it, in the bleakest of the novels with its victory of evil over good, in terms that show how urgent it was to find in literature a magic spell that would make the class conflict appear unreal.

Raabe appeared fully to share the view of Naturalism held by these spokesmen for his public. Especially in his private comments he spoke dismissively of the Naturalists and with particular bitterness of Ibsen (Sammons 1987, 159-60). But for two reasons modern observers have found this a little odd. First of all, among the Naturalists there were enthusiastic admirers of Raabe. For example, in 1886 Hermann Conradi, reviewing *Unruhige Gäste*, praised him as romantic and realist simultaneously (16: 549-50). In 1889 the Naturalist organ *Die Gesellschaft* fulsomely praised, of all things, *Der Hungerpastor* (6: 491-92). Arno Holz corresponded with Raabe, Heinrich Hart wrote a friendly review of *Gutmanns Reisen*, and in 1906, as we learn from Raabe's unpublished diary, Gerhart Hauptmann and Wilhelm Bölsche sent seventy-fifth birthday greetings from Hauptmann's estate (Sammons 1987, 159-60).

Secondly, Raabe was a constant reader of the *bête noir* for all poetic realists, the arch-Naturalist Emile Zola, to whom he seems to have paid an unusual amount of attention (Lensing 1988). An argument can be made that Raabe's late fiction represents a bridge between mid-century realism and Naturalism. What this muddle suggests is that his incomplete but addictive symbiosis with his public sometimes clouded his judgment about himself. The problem with Naturalism is not the only aspect of his career upon which this observation can be made.

The praise of Raabe at the expense of the Naturalists is a marker of his greatly improved reputation in the last decades of his life. If the terms of Raabe criticism remained disconcertingly static, its evaluative judgments were more variable. With his first work, *Die Chronik der Sperlingsgasse,* he achieved a *succès d'estime* that may well have been the impetus to his determination to devote his life to the writing of fiction. That a writer of the stature of Friedrich Hebbel, then in the prime of his career, should have taken note of it must have been intensely gratifying (1: 436-37). The response to his second novel, *Ein Frühling,* was also encouraging. But here already was an ominous sign of the gap that was to open between author and public. Unlike the *Chronik, Ein Frühling* has not had an enduring reputation. Raabe himself came to be embarrassed by it and tried to rewrite it beginning in 1865-66, completing the revision in 1870. This is the only time that he completely rewrote any of his works; the case reminds us of Gottfried Keller's repudiation of the first version of *Der grüne Heinrich* of 1855 and preparation of a thoroughly revised second version in 1889-90, right down to the effort of both authors to eradicate the first edition by acquiring and burning it. But, unlike Keller, Raabe did not improve the novel by revising it, nor did he himself think that he had done so. The second version remains obscure, as it has not yet appeared in the modern standard edition.

With the satirical dimension and narrator of doubtful status and dignity of *Die Kinder von Finkenrode,* Raabe took another step toward the discovery of his own voice. But with this experiment he ran directly into the refusal of critics to tolerate or even acknowledge experiments; the complaints about mixed levels of style, absence of form, obscurity, caricature, grotesqueness, mannerisms — in short, all the "Jean-Paulian" misdemeanors — begin in earnest. For years Raabe tried to find the formula that would be both true to himself and acceptable to his public, while the critics paid relatively little attention. However, one of them, Otto Banck, commenting on *Die Leute aus dem Walde* in 1864, warned, not without reason, that Raabe was writing too much too fast (5: 450-51). But if he was to keep pursuing his discordant purposes he had little choice.

A major crisis in his relationship with his public occurred during his Stuttgart period, when he invested every resource he could muster into three major novels, *Der Hungerpastor*, *Abu Telfan*, and *Der Schüdderump*, only to see them fail one after the other; even *Der Hungerpastor*, in the course of time his most famous, or notorious, work, had a slow start. Indeed, it was characteristic of his career that many of his works began to be critically appreciated years after they had been published, sometimes in response to new editions. *Abu Telfan*, however, never reached in his lifetime the relatively high standing it has obtained among critics today. This experience reinforced more or less permantly his bitter feelings about his relationship with his public. It also turned him away from the novel for some years, as he realized that he could earn more, page for page, with novellas and stories. The 1870s, a time of economic turmoil, were not good years for the fortunes of literature in general, and were probably Raabe's most frustrating decade, even as he continued regularly to produce works of, if anything, increasingly fine quality.

Sometime in the eighties criticism became friendlier, or at least more varied. This tendency continued through the following decade, as we begin to witness the republication in new editions, sometimes in considerable numbers, of works that had been long dormant. His sixtieth birthday in 1891 was celebrated quite energetically by his admirers. They put on another festival in 1894 for the fortieth anniversary of the day he began to write the *Chronik;* he was already beginning to enter the celebratory, ritualistic phase of his reputation. Despite his disinclination to look on the bright side of his fate, he could not fail to notice the change. At the end of 1892 he agreed that a younger generation of readers between twenty and thirty-five was beginning to discover him (E 2: 336-37), and in 1899 he is said to have remarked to a visitor: "Sehen Sie ..., die anderen gehen nun zu Bette — und ich — steh' nun auf" (E 4: 139). In that same year he was decorated with the Bavarian *Maxi-*

miliansorden as successor to the deceased Conrad Ferdinand Meyer. Thus the most spectacular turning point in his reputation, the elaborate seventieth-birthday celebration in 1901, when he was showered with praise, congratulations, honorary doctorates, and whatnot, did not occur so abruptly as may have appeared at the time.

By then a distinctly nationalist note had begun to establish itself in the criticism. More seriously, it has been suggested that the improvement in his reputation was owing to a desire in his public to cling to anti-modern tradition and old-fashioned values (Heim 1953, 284-88). In the critical materials there is a good deal of evidence, apart from the disparagement of Naturalism, that this was so. A reviewer of *Hastenbeck* in 1898 commented that the "durch und durch unmoderne Erzähler" had surprisingly become a "Modedichter" (20: 434). Similar comments appeared frequently in the late phase. Raabe never thought of himself as a conservative or programmatically old-fashioned writer, and this sort of commentary, along with the circumstance that it was often the earlier works, which he himself respected least, that were revived and began to roll up numerous editions, shows that it was not merely contrariness that caused him to be somewhat less than fulfilled by his late success. He was still dogged by misunderstanding and a failure of criticism to meet his estimate of himself.

Perhaps needless to say, the criticism that accompanied Raabe's career is not an unbroken record of solecism and blindness. Everywhere one encounters moments of insight, thoughtfully formulated observations, efforts to grasp his purposes rather than measure the texts by norms alien to them. Sometimes the best or at least best formulated criticism came from other writers, suggesting that he was in fact a writer's writer; for Raabe, who took practically no interest in his German literary environment, this would have been another sign of failure, for his aspiration was to be a writer of and for the people. The most thoughtful observation in the materials known to me was made in a review of a decade of work from *Pfisters Mühle* to *Stopfkuchen* by Karl Alberti in 1891, observing that Raabe forces his reader to intellectual effort along with him and makes of the reader a passive poet (17: 419). Leo Berg, about whom more will be said in the next chapter, made an equally perceptive comment on *Hastenbeck* in 1898: "Raabe gehört selbst zur Handlung.... Sein Realismus [hat] suggestive Gewalt auf den

Leser, dem er seine Menschen und Schicksale vor die Füße rollt, daß er sie aufheben muß, wenn er nicht über sie stolpern will" (20: 437). But such flashes of insight and eloquence are rare. Most readers did not want to be challenged to intellectual labor; they wanted to be reinforced in what they already knew and believed, and so also did the critics, who understood their office as articulating "what the public would have to say were it in a position to speak" (Hohendahl 1988, 215). Thus Raabe's posthumous reputation, for all the momentum it had gained during the last three decades of his life, became the possession of a public that was enthusiastic but poorly prepared.

2: The Era of the Cult

SHORTLY AFTER OUR AUTHOR'S DEATH on November 15, 1910, a group of his friends began to form an organization called "Die Gesellschaft der Freunde Wilhelm Raabes." This initiative certainly seems to have been timely, for it was an almost instant success. In 1911 the Raabe-Gesellschaft began to publish a newsletter, the *Mitteilungen*, which for years was the main vehicle of discourse about the writer. The society came to be organized in chapters throughout Germany and grew to be, after the Goethe-Gesellschaft, the second-largest literary society in the country. On the one hand, the Raabe-Gesellschaft in its proselytizing zeal probably expanded the popular readership of Raabe to its feasible limits, and in that sense was certainly pursuing one of the author's goals, so long frustrated in his lifetime. But, on the other hand, it clamped a proprietary hold on his reception, reshaped him and his texts to suit their own preoccupations, stifled variety of opinion and, indeed, in a certain sense, criticism altogether, and ultimately carried him with it into the epochal disaster into which the German petty-bourgeoisie ran itself. While this episode is now purely historical, with practically no influence on the current discourse about Raabe, it constitutes a large block in the history of his reception, giving to it an ominous, singular, yet historically significant shape.

However, the Raabe-Gesellschaft did not establish its hegemony instantaneously. While in some ways its discourse is a continuation of the criticism that accompanied Raabe's career, especially extending the shallowness and complacency characteristic of the latter decades of it, other, more modern initiatives had begun to develop that emerged for a time outside of or peripheral to the orthodox community. Therefore, before turning to the "criticism" that developed under the aegis of the Raabe-Gesellschaft, we may look at some critical beginnings that emerged earlier.

a: The Pre-Cult Window

Raabe's attitude toward discourse about him was consistent and crystal clear. While destructive or rejectionist criticism angered and sometimes discouraged him, and he was often exasperated by its obtuseness and refusal of perception, he benignly welcomed well-meant criticism regardless of how adequate it appeared to him. To be sure, when it was not well-meant, he could become quite testy. In 1910 he was particularly outraged by a condescending and belittling segment on him in Richard M[oritz] Meyer's *Die deutsche Literatur des Neunzehnten Jahrhunderts* (Meyer 1912 [originally 1910], 354-59), which was to become one of the standard literary histories of the age. Meyer even called Raabe's patriotism into question for not fully accepting the wonders and promise of the Wilhelminian Reich, and that was not a charge that he was likely to regard with equanimity. He repeatedly grouched about this *blamage*, twice forgetting himself so far as to refer to the Jewish scholar as "Richard Moses Meyer" (E 2: 412, 416, 418, 420). But he was unfailingly courteous and grateful to his public supporters; he made no effort to control the discourse, as he was in general very parsimonious in offering interpretive aids; and he willingly recognized that there could be differences in interpretation and understanding, including differences from his own understanding of what he had intended and accomplished. The founders of the Raabe-Gesellschaft might have reasonably been confident that the undertaking was in the master's spirit and one that would have gratified him.

At the same time he systematically discouraged any inquiry into his life and person; deflected all queries about the "real" models of his fictional characters, locations, and events; and insisted again and again that such matters were not interesting or important and those wishing truly to know him should read (and buy, though he did not put it that way) his books. He evaded almost all requests for autobiographical memoirs, and the little he did supply is terse and unrevealing. He did what he could to hinder biographical writing about him by others. This stance does not imply that he had something to hide, at least not any more than is customary in the human psyche. He was by nature reticent and introverted, as many North Germans are. It is quite true that he did not lead a very interesting life. In fact, though many people were charmed by him in varying degrees, he was not really a very interesting person. He relentlessly focused all the energies of his being on the writing of fiction, and it was by the creative results that he wished to be known. This self-circumscription his followers found difficult to accept. Perhaps the reason is that Raabe the man was more like them, as he had been among his *Stammtisch* entourage during his lifetime, while Raabe the artist, about whom he rarely deigned to speak, and then only cryptically, was beyond their horizon of perception. Thus the worship of the man came to flatten and trivialize the discourse about the works. In any case, the result was that descriptive and interpretive studies of his writing began to emerge during his lifetime, while the first biographical monograph could appear only after his death.

The best example of Raabe's attitude toward favorable criticism is the interest he took in the first interpretive book written about him, Paul Gerber's *Wilhelm Raabe: Eine Würdigung seiner Dichtungen,* published in Leipzig in 1897. Gerber, a "professor" (that is, a high-ranking schoolteacher) in Stargard in Pomerania, had already published an anonymous essay on *Stopfkuchen* in 1891; from the moment that Raabe had learned that Gerber was its author and was intending to continue writing about him, he encouraged him consistently, beginning in early 1893 (E 2: 340); gave him every assistance, including providing a photograph (E 2: 387, not used in the book); praised the work when it came out (E 2: 390-91); and remained in friendly contact with him until his death in 1909, on which occasion he sent a heartfelt letter of condolence to the widow (*"In alls gedultig"* 404-05). I imagine that he felt this sort of publication about him was a form of recognition of him as a literary figure; to be written about critically is to be canonized, and there can be no doubt that Raabe aspired to a place in the canon of remembered German writers. To Gerber he wrote:

> Abgesehen von jeder Kritik meinerseits im Einzelnen, ist mir Ihr Buch als Ganzes eine solche Bürgschaft dafür, daß eine mehr als vierzigjährige Lebensarbeit nicht umsonst gethan worden ist, daß es allein schon des Lohnes genug ist. (E 2: 395).

For it must have been Gerber's good intentions more than his critical acumen that beguiled Raabe. In fact, right at the outset of their correspondence, he gently hinted that Gerber had missed the symbolic dimension of *Stopfkuchen* (E 2: 340). He dropped another hint concerning his good opinion of *Zum wilden Mann* that Gerber declined to take; instead, reflecting the conventional response, he rejected it on the grounds that its bitter spirit was incompatible with literature (Gerber 1897, 186). Raabe was careful to mention that, though Gerber was the first, another might come who would see things differently (E 2: 395).

The book itself need not detain us very long. In insight it is not much of an advance over the journalistic criticism of the time, having as an advantage only the perspective over the whole career (except *Hastenbeck*, which had not yet appeared). For the most part, it alternates fulsome praise with plot summaries. In the spirit of the times, it begins with a nationalistic tirade, denouncing the Socialists as enemies of true culture and praising Bismarck and Kaiser Wilhelm I (Gerber 1897, 4-5). It sets Raabe in opposition to modern literature, which no one needs: "Was sollen die ästhetischen Spiele mit Gefühlen und Formen?" (17). Gerber speaks constantly of Raabe's humor as a victory over loss, suffering, and death, sometimes incongruously. Of *St. Thomas* he writes:

> Der Dichter löst diese Widersprüche auf, indem er die Dinge in seine Sphäre hinaufhebt. Er zeigt das Erhebende, das oft auch im Schmerz liegt (59) —

a comment that seems to me ill-suited to the foregrounded futility of the slaughter and suffering in that work. Like many of those fixated on this line, he is uneasy at the genuinely comic works such as *Die Gänse von Bützow*, yet he finds kind words to say about it, as well as about *Der Dräumling* and even *Christoph Pechlin*, which many Raabe admirers have not much liked (253-301). He differs further from the conventional line by defending the narratively experimental structure of *Drei Federn* (142-43), and he stresses the compositional skills of a writer often charged with formlessness (313). Despite his nationalistic prologue, he acknowledges the tolerance of *Deutscher Adel* (194), which, notwithstanding its title, is one of the most cosmopolitan in spirit of Raabe's works.

But what differentiates Gerber's approach from what was to come more than anything else is that he also criticizes aspects of Raabes œuvre. It is not so much a matter of how pertinent the criticisms themselves look to us today, as that he criticizes at all, for differentiated evaluation was largely suppressed in the era of the cult. But his grounds for criticism are not uninteresting, for they show Gerber to be more a man of his own time than his diatribe against literary modernism would indicate. For example, he rejects *Das letzte Recht* because it has confused superstition with poesy, and even objects that Raabe allowed the novella to be twice anthologized (138-39). In regard to *Pfisters Mühle* Gerber defends the possibilities of technology against what he takes to be Raabe's attack on it; although he has doubtlessly misread the novel, it is noteworthy that he believes that an unjust critique of technology would destroy the ideals of the future (228-29). He finds Raabe too backward looking and worries that if we listen to Wachholder in the *Chronik* we will turn backwards ourselves. He praises the author for his depictions of city life, his lack of euphemism, his representation of the ugly and the narrow (331), characteristics that were usually charged against the despised Naturalists. But his resignation — what is customarily referred to in criticism as "pessimism" — is contrary to the spirit of hope of modern culture. Thus Gerber as an optimistic citizen of the thriving Wilhelminian Reich implicitly denies Raabe the dignity of prophecy. Again it is not so much the quality of his criticism as its relative independence that must strike us in retrospect.

Another critic who caught Raabe's eye was Leo Berg (1862-1908), whose essay on his career in a book called *Aus der Zeit — gegen die Zeit* (1905) he noted with gratitude in a letter (E 2: 462). He owned this and two other of Berg's books, including *Neue Essays* of 1901 (Bänsch 1970, 95), which, according to a note in his copy, he also acquired in 1905 and which contained an essay of 1897 on "Wilhelm Raabe als Erzähler" and a review of *Hastenbeck* originally published in 1899. Here was a critic of a higher calibre than Gerber or the common run of journalistic reviewers, a literary essayist by profession with a colorful style. He is also another example of the one-way relationship of the Naturalists with Raabe, for he was a co-founder of the *Verein Durch* and the *Freie Bühne* in Berlin. He observed that Raabe was not a popular writer, and was one of those who warned perceptively that his community of admirers could be dangerous to him by cutting him off from the larger public (Berg 1901, 269). Berg commented thoughtfully on Raabe's characterization, his relationship to history, and his sense of tragedy, and remarked acutely that *Else von der Tanne*, then little noted but subsequently to become much more highly regarded, was one of his most powerful and personal stories and a prefiguration in tone of *Der Schüdderump* (270, 273). Berg at least adumbrated Raabe's literary-historical placement, arching over the era of the programmatic realism: he "steht mit beiden Füßen in der Romantik, während sein Haupt in eine neue Zeit hineinragt, und so ist er zwiefach *unzeitgemäß*" (278). But it was on Raabe's narration that he came to what were for his time the most original results, remarking (with some exaggeration) that most of his characters have no clear physiognomy and individuality, only the narrator does, and that he relates not a story but his sympathy with the story (279, 283). In conclusion he compared Raabe's self-irony to Ibsen's (283), a point that Raabe himself would have been incapable of seeing. In the *Hastenbeck* review Berg argues that Raabe symbolizes the same concept of inescapable fate that we find in a technological-scientific form in Zola. Thus Berg was another one of those who shows how anxious the Naturalists were to claim Raabe as their own, as much as he may have resisted the abduction.

Leo Berg was Jewish. The Jewish reception of Raabe is an unresearched topic, but it might bear some attention, especially as the greatest single problem in the history of his reputation is that his eventually most widely read work, *Der Hungerpastor*, acquired the odium of an anti-Semitic novel. We would likely find that the view of many Jews of the time of *Der Hungerpastor*, as of Gustav Freytag's similarly problematic *Soll und Haben*, was rather different from our own, and that Raabe had a good many Jewish admirers in spite of the presence of rabid anti-Semites like Adolf Bartels in his circle of acquaintance and among his more trivial critics. An early example was a Viennese Jew named Josef Bass, who wrote a long essay on Raabe's Jewish figures that he had intended to present to the author on his eightieth birthday, but, when Raabe died first, printed in a Jewish monthly in 1910. Bass reviews a long list of sympathetic portrayals of Jewish figures in Raabe's œuvre and defends *Der Hungerpastor* partly on typological grounds, partly on the ground that so wise a man could not despise a whole class of human beings (Bass 1910, 655). In another place Bass was to say that *Der Hungerpastor* was one of the early reading experiences that had made him an admirer of Raabe (Bass 1912,

129). Bass (1910, 667) also criticized Marie Speyer for seeing *Hollunderblüte* as concerned with the Jewish problem.

Originally from Luxemberg, she was the author of the first dissertation on Raabe, published in Regensburg in 1908. However, very few German universities even admitted women at that time, and I assume that the dissertation was written at Freiburg in Switzerland, where her director, Wilhelm Kosch, was then professor. Bass, in any case, must have misunderstood her, for she says that Raabe in *Hollunderblüte* is less interested in the Jewish-Christian contrast than in the universally human aspect and the social and cultural gap between the characters (Speyer 1908, 21). Her dissertation was no more than a workmanlike achievement; it is notable because it was the first and because it appeared during the lifetime of the author, who wrote warmly to her as well as to Professor Kosch (E 2: 481, 482). Speyer became a welcome figure in the Raabe community and published on him from time to time in later years.

The second dissertation was completed at the University of Bonn in the last year of Raabe's life: Hermann Junge, *Wilhelm Raabe: Studien über Form und Inhalt seiner Werke.* This, too, is a study of some promise. Junge gives attention to structure, pointing out in one place that Raabe hides the main structural lines by giving an illusion of "Willkürlichkeit und Absichtslosigkeit" (Junge 1910, 35), and also makes some observations on narrative perspective. He comments on the leanness of Raabe's description; on the one hand, he interestingly concludes from this that Raabe's writing is not "Heimatkunst" (41), but, on the other, criticizes him for his preoccupation with inner processes at the expense of the setting (60). Junge rightly observes that Raabe came to differentiate characters less by class origin than by *Weltanschauung,* and that there was a more democratic spirit in his earliest works (117). Concerning the much bruited influence of Jean Paul he ventures a succinct judgment: "Seinen Einfluß auf Raabe möchte ich nicht so gering, wie Raabe selbst ..., aber nicht so hoch, wie einige seiner Beurteiler anschlagen" (132), a judicious formulation with which I think most of today's Raabe scholars would agree. Raabe is said to have reacted to this study, a mere ten days before his death, with his customary delight: "Jetzt werde ich nun schon bei lebendigem Leibe auf der Universität in Seminar- und Doktorarbeiten anatomisch zergliedert" (E 4: 312). Unfortunately, the promise suggested by this effort was not sustained. Junge, who evidently became a clergyman, in later occasional essays continuing well into the Nazi period, was one of those who, against all evidence, tried to portray Raabe as a Christian *quand même* (Junge 1912a, 1912b, 1931, 1938); it seems as though the ambience of the Raabe-Gesellschaft could blunt a critical edge that had once been present.

While Raabe offered to interpreters of his writing little help but much encouragement, to would-be biographers he offered neither help nor encouragement. He seems to have been virtually traumatized by the consequences of having revealed, early in his career in 1861, something of his person and inner life to a journalist named Thaddäus Lau (E 2: 66-68); motifs from these informal musings echoed in commentary about him for years, making him very irritable. Thereafter it was his practice to repel biographical inquiry with blunt words. By the end of his life he knew that he could not ban biography forever, but he could prevent it from appearing in his lifetime. Thus the first genuine biography, Herm[an] Anders Krüger, *Der junge Raabe: Jugendjahre und Erstlingswerke*, did not appear until 1911, though it had been composed several years earlier. Krüger (1871-1945) was a writer of some success in his time, though today totally forgotten; he was also the author of an excellent, still useful biographical dictionary, *Deutsches Literatur-Lexikon* (Munich: Beck, 1914). Having been writing occasionally about Raabe since 1893, Krüger gained access to him in 1903 and in 1906 read a drama he had written on Frederick the Great to Raabe and his friends; later he was to be the representative of the *Deutscher Schriftsteller-Verband* at Raabe's funeral (Spiero 1931, 132; E 4: 203-04, 229-30, 318-19). Apparently at the turn of the years 1909/09 he sent Raabe a draft of an account of the author's origins and early years. Raabe replied demanding that it not be published in his lifetime, to which Krüger readily agreed — no great sacrifice, perhaps, since Raabe was seventy-seven years old and visibly aging. In a further letter he said such a work would make him feel that he had gone out in public in his underwear, an image he also employed in an insistence to Professor Kosch, who seems to have been Krüger's go-between, that the book must not appear (E 2: 484-85). He then chided Krüger for exhibiting the impatience of the age, the inability to wait and allow things to mature, and hinted that the draft was full of errors, which he promised to deal with in conversation (Hoppe 1963, 53-54; also Hoppe 1967, 67-68). Thus *Der junge Raabe* was not published until 1911.

Raabe must have straightened out whatever errors may have been in the draft, for Krüger's book makes an eminently accurate impression. It is, in fact, the foundation of our knowledge about Raabe's beginnings. If today it reads somewhat redundantly for the specialist, it is because his factual materials have become common knowledge for us. Krüger also attempts a critical overview of the works through *Die Kinder von Finkenrode*, including the first novella collection, *Halb Mähr, halb mehr*, of 1859. His criticism is plausible if not memorable, but it contains a number of features that make it stand out in contrast to what was soon to come. What he has to say about Raabe's formative literary influences shows every sign of having come directly from the author's mouth. He mentions Balzac as an influence, which, to my knowledge, no subsequent critic did, and puts particular stress on the significance of Thackeray as a model (Krüger 1911, 34, 67-72), adding the suggestion that someone should write a genuinely comparative study of Raabe and Thackeray (144), a task that has not been fully discharged to this day. At the same time Krüger minimized the influence of Dickens and Jean Paul, and of Schopenhauer on Raabe's "pessimism" (36-37), while pointing out his admiration of Heine, "so sonderbar es vielleicht manchem erscheinen will" (35), a point that the cultists were wont to suppress. Krüger gives a little attention to narrative technique, commenting on the complexity of time levels (75). It might also be mentioned that, although his origins were among the Moravian Brethren and his own writing was of a religious nature, he is completely tolerant of Raabe's religious indifference and does not try to pretend it was something else. But he is by no means uncritical. He sees the immature unevenness in the *Chronik* (78-85) and mounts a thoughtful comparison of the two versions of *Ein Frühling*, clearly recognizing the revision as a failure but adding not unjustly that the novel "auch unüberarbeitet kein einwandfreies Kunstwerk war" (114). The book concludes with a bibliography of Raabe's works and of the secondary literature up to that time, the latter prefaced with a judicious and slightly acerbic commentary on the then current state of criticism (169-71).

Krüger, incidentally, does not seem to have maintained a close connection with the Raabe-Gesellschaft. His couple of essays in later years were published outside it. His memoir of meeting Raabe, included in a centennial Festschrift sponsored by the Raabe-Gesellschaft, was taken from an autobiography previously published (Spiero 1931, 132-34). It would be interesting to know whether Krüger consciously absented himself from the cult, and if so, why.

b: Captured by the "Friends"

Several efforts were made to organize groups of Raabe admirers during his lifetime; he looked upon them benignly, as he did on all signs of interest in him, but they were not sustained (Denkler 1987a, 14). In February 1911 some 300 members of an originally liberal club in Braunschweig called the *Kleiderseller* founded the society of friends. The "friendship" was a little aggrandized. It is true that the founders and leaders of the Raabe-Gesellschaft tended to be people who had known him personally. However, Raabe's attachment to the *Kleiderseller* had been a matter of the 1870s and 1880s; later he gravitated to another, less bourgeois and more artistic club, *Der feuchte Pinsel*. A school official named Wilhelm Brandes (1854-1928) made himself officially Raabe's closest friend, jostling aside another candidates for this honor, including a rather miffed Wilhelm Jensen (15, 17). From the outset Brandes, who was president until 1926, insisted on exclusive proprietary rights to Raabe. A rival group, the *Raabe-Bund*, led by the journalist and author Otto Elster (1852-1922) and his son Hanns Martin Elster (b. 1888), though it managed to put out issues of a *Wilhelm Raabe Kalender* in Berlin for the years 1912, 1913, and 1914 (Elster and Elster 1911, 1912, 1913), was so vigorously attacked by the Raabe-Gesellschaft that it gave up and dissolved itself. In 1912 the society pursued a fiery feud with the *Frankfurter Zeitung*, which had printed an account of Raabe that made him look less like an iconic model figure and more like a real, quirky person skeptical of pomposity (Denkler 1987a, 18-19). Brandes, an indefatigable propagandist, defined from the outset the anti-critical and anti-aesthetic bias of the Raabe-Gesellschaft, claiming that Raabe himself had insisted it be unscholarly (E 4: 296). Well before Raabe's death and the founding of the society, Brandes had written that

> die Kreise, die Keller oder Storm oder Mörike verehren, haben doch alle im wesentlichen einen ästhetischen, die Raabegemeinde allein hat einen ganz überwiegend ethischen Charakter. Sie bildet, wenn man den Ausdruck recht verstehen will, eine Sekte, eine Freimauerei ... durch alles Volk deutscher Zunge daheim und draußen weit in der Diaspora. (Brandes 1906, 34)

Russell Berman has remarked on an "an anti-critical bias within the culture of [German] realism," and in Naturalism as well (Hohendahl 1988, 278, 298), but the posture of the Raabe-Gesellschaft in this regard was especially pronounced. It was extremely hostile to criticism emerging from outside its ranks. An example was a Freiburg dissertation by Herbert Schiller, published in 1917, which aroused the ire of the "friends" (Denkler 1987a, 20-21). In 1921 Brandes was still raging against "eine neunmal gescheite Überästhetik" (Bauer and Schultz 1921, 39); a decade after it was published it was bitterly attacked in the *Mitteilungen* (Zornemann 1927), and the assault continued into the mid-1930s (Denkler 1987a, 20). When in 1912 one Hans Naumann, on the occasion of dedicating a monument to Raabe in Braunschweig, gave a speech that made it sound too much as though the author had been a figure of the past, he was severely taken to task several years later by one of the stalwarts, who remarked that one could not expect an admirer of Thomas Mann to have the right view of Raabe (Naumann 1932; *Mitt.* 25 [1936]: 132). Hostility to Thomas Mann is a leitmotif of the "friends" in the inter-war years, a sign both of their anti-modernism and their revulsion at Mann's support of the Weimar Republic. In itself the monograph is no loss; Schiller was a glib Beckmesser who measured Raabe by rigid notions of aesthetics appropriate to the epic genre drawn from Goethean classicism and intermixed with the "objective" narrative theory against which Raabe's œuvre was oriented from the outset. But it is not merely the negative evaluation that is unacceptable, but also the attempt at formal and aesthetic analysis; Raabe's friends see him as a "Führer durchs Leben" rather than an artist, while the aesthetically oriented reader cannot perceive him this way (Zornemann 1927, 137). More unreasonable was the attack from within the community on the much more substantial study of Nicolaas Perquin, about which there will be more to say farther along. Here the objection was to an analysis that appeared to challenge Brandes's gospel about the consistent unity of Raabe's *Weltanschauung* (Westerburg 1931, 152).

The influence of the society reached into academic study. An example is a Marburg dissertation of 1918 on *Die Akten des Vogelsangs,* again by a woman, Margarete Bönneken. She takes an extremely nationalistic tone from the outset, paralleling Raabe with the chauvinist race theorist Paul de Lagarde. One of the basic conflicts in the novel is defined "im Völkischen: Deutschland gegen Amerika" (Bönneken 1926 [originally 1918], 27). Raabe's "Innerlichkeit" is contrasted with the "wichtigtuende und gefällige Selbstbeobachtung, wie sie wohl moderne Literaten zeigen" (55), an observation that strikes us as ironic today, when Raabe's self-consciousness as a narrator is seen as one of his proto-modern aspects. She comments on Just Everstein in *Alte Nester:* "Er ist zugleich Träger deutscher Bildung, deutschen Wesens, wir würden ihn heute einen Wegbereiter des Auslandsdeutschtums nennen" (97), although the text makes it explicit that Everstein has outgrown his German diffidence and vagueness in America, where he has acquired the self-confidence and independence that enable him to be successful upon his return. She mounts an elaborate attack on the suggestion that Raabe might have admired Heine (167-72), although Krüger had known this was true ten years earlier. The dissertation contains ominous signs of what was to come. It was widely admired among the "friends" as a shining example of criticism, and Bönneken was virtually beatified after she died in 1919 (death notice *Mitt.* 10 [1920]: 35; see also Fehse 1921). The dissertation was republished in 1926 and, superfluously, in 1968. Today a not unreasonable evaluation of it would be "worthless."

The adulation of Raabe by the "friends" often looks like the self-adulation of the petty-bourgeois subclass that constituted the bulk of the society. They praised themselves as "Raabemenschen," a type of model German, more inward, more transcendentally oriented, more sensitive, more humorous, more idealistic than the common run of mankind. A statement of the Düsseldorf chapter in 1924 is not untypical of the tone:

> Was in uns denkt, im Tiefsten fühlt und strebt, wollen wir
> in schönen Stunden der Gemeinsamkeit fest auf den Meister
> hinrichten, in ihm, dem Unerschöpflichen, uns sammeln
> und erhöhen, ja uns *finden*.... Kurz, wir wollen in Raabe uns
> *selbst*: unser verborgen Wesen und Leben, unsere, durch
> den äußeren Tag nie befriedigte, weil zeitüberlegene
> Innerlichkeit. (*Mitt.* 14 [1924]: 26)

From the outset the "Raabemenschen" were exceptionally class-conscious. Brandes linked them to the master through the quality of "Gemüt," which only the middle class possessed and which he defined as

> das tiefe und innige Gefühl für die ethischen Werte
> und Bindungen des Lebens, ein Gefühl, das auf
> Ahnung und Einsicht ruhend sich aus Liebe und
> Ehrfucht mischt. (Brandes 1906, 76-77, 71)

As a consequence the documents intermittently contain disdainful remarks about the Social Democrats and the working class generally. Raabe was raised to virtually messianic heights: Wilhelm Fehse, of whom more presently, asked rhetorically: "Sähen wir nicht in ihm den höchsten Parakleten unseres Volkes, wo wäre dann unsere Raabe-Gesellschaft" (Fehse 1921, 51), an echo of a scrap of one of the pompous speeches at the Schiller centenary in *Der Dräumling*: "Er lebe hoch als Freund und als Vorbild, der Paraklet unseres, des Beraters, Helfers, Vermittlers oft so bedürftigen Volkes!" (10: 119).

To be sure, such worshipful congregations are not unknown to the history of literature. A comparison valuable for demonstrating cultural similarities and differences might someday be mounted between the Raabe-Gesellschaft and the Browning Society, which was founded in 1881, while the poet was still alive. Browning looked upon it with a bemused gratification similar to Raabe's attitude toward efforts on his behalf; like Raabe, he was "uniformly gracious to his admirers, no matter how misguided they might be" (Peterson 1969, 95). The motivation was similar also: the feeling that Browning was undervalued by the public and deserved a more prominent standing in the life of the nation. Very much like Raabe, Browning was distressed by "the fickleness of popular judgment, or, as he phrased it himself in *The Ring and the Book*, with the 'British Public, ye who like me not'" (6). This society also took on cultic aspects, inclining to extravagant claims for Browning's prophetic and salvationary authority bearing "a message from heaven to an unbelieving and materialistic age" (4), while displaying much evidence that his texts were often beyond the acolytes' understanding. The view of him that he was "a poet possessing a great message yet so inarticulate that his ideas had to be interpreted to the world" (11) is not so different from the practice of extracting Raabe's message by suppressing attention to its fictive and imaginative vehicle. Brandes, for example, described the impatient reader of Raabe's style working through "einen selbstwachsenen Eichenkamp, das oben seine Zweige, unten seine Wurzeln verschränkt, und allerlei häkelndes Unterholz" (Brandes 1906, 101). A comparable disinclination to literary criticism marked most of the discourse, which was more concerned to reiterate generalizations and encomia; one of the regulars "was strongly opposed to any sort of analysis of Browning's poetry, for that might lead to adverse criticism of it, which in turn could cause one to neglect its great spiritual lessons which Browning had provided for one's personal guidance" (Peterson 1969, 88). Even more than the Raabe-Gesellschaft, the Browning Society attracted religious enthusiasts determined to explicate his message as one of Christian renewal; this was a version of the anti-modern affect very prominent among the "Raabemenschen" also, and contrasts in the same way to the tendency of later criticism to detect modern elements in Browning. The Browningites also elevated their self-esteem by mirroring themselves in the master; its evangelism "began to marvel at the contrast between its own purity of spirit and the dark, polluted world where Browning's spiritual message had not penetrated" (135). As in Raabe's case, the passage of time turned the organization from an asset to the master's reputation into a liability: "in our own century Browning's readers have, almost without exception, regarded the Browning Society as a dead albatross hung around his neck" (189).

There were also significant differences. Although the Raabe-Gesellschaft endured some internal disputes — for instance, concerning the publication of Raabe's texts in abridged form for less demanding readers — the Browning Society had disputatiousness built into it, as it "harbored all manner of dissenters ... a microcosm of the London literary world, in which every variety of attitude toward Browning's poetry was expressed" (4). All sorts of incongruous people are found in it, among them George Bernard Shaw, who seems to have attended the meetings primarily to make fun of the others, and Karl Marx's daughter Eleanor. Some of the founders were as militantly agnostic as some of the followers were pious, and indeed it was largely these religious disputes that caused the society to dissolve itself in 1892, though segments of it continue to live on even today in England and in America. Furthermore, although there was some criticism of the Raabe-Gesellschaft from the outside, there was nothing in Germany to compare to the relentless lampooning and caricature to which the Browningites were subjected — it "must have been the most satirized institution in England" (173). This is, of course, a difference in cultural tone, but beyond that it indicates that the "Raabemenschen" were more representative of a larger national constituency than the Browningites were.

William S. Peterson has pointed out that, notwithstanding the extensive case that can be made against the Browning Society today, it did have its worthwhile side. It undertook positivistic researches and formed a ground for later scholarship; it "had some connection with nearly every book about Browning published between 1881 and the end of the century," with the consequence that "Browning's poetry has received the kind of detailed study and explication that has been accorded few other writers of the Victorian period" (166). The Raabe-Gesellschaft, too, had its productive aspects. In the midst of all the unction, a significant amount of research was accomplished, which appears in bits and pieces, along with a certain amount of reasonable commentary, in the *Mitteilungen*. In 1925, Constantin Bauer, one of the noblest of the "friends," as we shall see, re-edited the first ten years of the *Mitteilungen*, excising the chaff in favor of the more substantial contributions, one of which actually devalues Raabe's best seller, *Der Hungerpastor*, in favor of *Der Schüdderump* (Bauer 1925, 212-38). Sponsoring volumes of collected commentary was a custom of the Raabe-Gesellschaft. In 1912 there appeared a *Gedächtnisschrift*, a combination of eulogies and text studies (Goebel 1912); it was revised in 1931, retaining a half-dozen of the original articles (one of them by Bass on Raabe's Jewish figures) and adding a number of new ones, including a reminiscence by Hermann Hesse of a visit to

Raabe (Goebel 1931). In 1921, for Raabe's ninetieth birthday, Bauer and Hans Martin Schultz edited a *Raabe-Gedenkbuch,* a by now familiar mix of reminiscences, encomia, newly found texts, and an occasional inquiring essay (Bauer and Schultz 1921). In 1931, Raabe's centenary, which was the occasion of a great outpouring of writing about him, Heinrich Spiero edited a Festschrift entitled *Wilhelm Raabe und sein Lebenskreis,* which includes, along some of the customary filler, reminiscences of Raabe's daughters, information on his social connections, and a series of genuinely useful articles about his closest acquaintances (Spiero 1931). In the same year Schultz published a critical bibliography of the secondary literature up to that time (Schultz 1931). Fritz Jensch (1879-1945) made a hobby of running down Raabe's innumerable allusions and quotations, literary and otherwise. In 1925 he published a whole book of them, *Wilhelm Raabes Zitatenschatz.* But there were many he could not identify, and he recurrently appealed to the membership for help (*Mitt.* 14 [1924]: 140-47; 16 [1926]: 204-07; 18 [1928]: 39-41; 19 [1929]: 87-92; 21 [1931]: 71-75). This game has not been played to the end to the present day. Furthermore, the Raabe-Gesellschaft was much more active than the Browning Society in collecting manuscripts, finding and publishing new texts, especially letters, and overseeing two complete editions, one in 1913-16, the other in 1934.

In addition, there was a certain amount of publication that appeared outside the circle of adepts. One of the more curious phenomena was a series of studies by Helene Dose, culminating in two books that placed Raabe in a mystical and arcane tradition (Dose 1925, 1928). The "friends" rejected this approach, and in this case they were right. Raabe's ideal is not mystical but stoic, and putting him into a mystical context is merely another way of forcing him into a religious posture.

Occasionally studies emerged in foreign countries. Since Raabe had thriven in translation primarily in Dutch, it seems fitting that two ambitious ones should emerge from the Netherlands. One of them, *Wilhelm Raabes Motive als Ausdruck seiner Weltan-schauung* of 1927 by Nicolaas Cornelis Adrianus Perquin S. J., a dissertation at the University of Amsterdam, is one of the most thoughtfully probing of the earlier studies. Much of it is, naturally, dated; it shows its origin in the age of *Geistesgeschichte* in its

pursuit of *Weltanschauung* without giving any attention to narrative devices. The main line is that the early works exhibit no
Weltanschauung but merely naive narration — Perquin adduces a
great many literary models, making Raabe look rather derivative
— and that he came to be preoccupied with the goal of harmony,
which, in its unrealizability, led to pessimism and the defeat of the
good, reaching a nadir in *Meister Autor* and *Zum wilden Mann*.
Perquin is quite good on the much threshed topic of pessimism,
ascribing it less to Schopenhauer's influence than to Raabe's
congenital disposition, and arguing that it is not a full or completed
pessimism, for Raabe seeks salvation in the imagination, in
interpersonal compassion, and in humor, in full awareness that
they are life's illusions:

> So kann man von einer Überwindung des Pessimismus
> reden, wenn man dabei nur nicht vergißt, daß diese
> Überwindung einer Inkonsequenz, einem Zwiespalt von
> Einsicht und Lebenstrieb, zu verdanken ist. (Perquin 1927,
> 209)

The great question governing Raabe's most mature works, Perquin
argues, is whether life is subject to blind fate or whether fate is
governed by a benign and intelligible providence (244). His
complex and somewhat obsessive pursuit of this question seems to
find that Raabe came to no clear conclusion. The fragmentary
Altershausen ends his career with a question mark (236), and Raabe
was unable to arrive at the place where his nature and his longings
directed him (294). Within this superintending argument there are
many acute and arresting local observations on particular texts and
problems.

However much we may agree or disagree with it in detail,
Perquin's study is one of the most alertly intelligent before the
contemporary phase of criticism. It makes much of the discourse
under the aegis of the Raabe-Gesellschaft seem naive and
provincial; indeed, early on Perquin comments on the one-
sidedness and excessive emotional dependence of the German
scholars (11). Yet it has been almost completely ignored in the
subsequent history of Raabe criticism. It is not surprising that, as I
noted above, the disciples did not much like it. Its effect is to make
Raabe appear complex, strained, contradictory, and at odds with
himself — all, of course, modern features incompatible with the

disciples' picture of him as a reliable wellspring of harmonious wisdom and guidance. It would be quite interesting to know why a Dutch Jesuit invested so much energy into an ultimately sympathetic study of the culturally Protestant, intellectually agnostic Raabe. A worthwhile task for one of today's scholars would be to find out more about Perquin.

A second Dutch dissertation, at the University of Nijmegen in 1930, was Friedrich Röttger's *Volk und Vaterland bei Wilhelm Raabe.* Anyone familiar with the nationalistic and chauvinistic excesses of the Raabe criticism of the past will find this title ominous, and will not be comforted by an acknowledgment of the aid of the Raabe-Gesellschaft. But, actually, though not brilliant, it is not as bad as one might think. Röttger, despite his German name, presents himself as a native Netherlander and rather oddly published the dissertation in Austria, in effect avoiding the *Vaterland.* His main purpose is to describe the historical environment of Raabe's works, so that the study might be valuable for students whose grasp of nineteenth-century German history may not be thorough. He gives a fair account of Raabe's nationalist, anti-particularist, *kleindeutsch,* pro-Bismarck allegiances, as well as his occasional allergy to foreign influences and interventions. But he also calls attention to some matters that the "friends" may have been less inclined to stress: Raabe's early opposition to reactionary government; his scorn for the aristocracy, which eased only later in life; his sense of class and sympathy for the proletariat; his concern for freedom. Röttger also highlights Raabe's refreshing lack of dynastic loyalty:

> Über die Herzöge von Braunschweig, mit Ausnahme des Herzogs Ferdinand [who was not a ruling duke], läßt Raabe sich nicht gerade in sehr schmeichelhafter Weise aus. (Röttger 1930, 279)

Röttger calls Raabe's position "idealdemokratisch," while recognizing that he, like many conservatives, believed that inner, individual freedom must be achieved before social freedom (346, 348-49). As for the Jews, Raabe regarded them as "Schicksalsgenossen des deutschen Volkes" (374). Röttger's most ingenious and remarkable result, however, does not lie within these matters, but in his computation that *Die Akten des Vogelsangs* is set in the future, in 1923 or 1918! (315-16). I was quite startled by this and thought about it a good deal before deciding that it could not be correct (see also Meinerts 1940, 217-18, n. 105). But it shows how an outsider might come up with a wholly new, unconventional idea. In any case, Röttger's study seems more sensible and humane than a Rostock dissertation published in 1926, Wilhelm Heess, *Raabe: Seine Zeit und seine Berufung*. This endeavor seems to owe much to Josef Nadler's effort to interpret German literature by its tribal character, which is amusing in view of Raabe's strong disinclination to be a "niedersächsischer Stammesdichter" (E 4: 179). Heess's obscurantist maunderings about poetry from the blood of the folk and the true word of the soul are of no interest other than as an ideological marker of their times.

The longest book ever written about Raabe in a foreign language appeared in French in 1939: Louis Kientz's *Wilhelm Raabe: L'homme, la pensée et l'œuvre*. In 1931 Kientz had reported in the *Mitteilungen* about French scholarship on Raabe, the magnitude of which he rather exaggerated. There has never been much interest in Raabe in France, even to the present day, and much of what there has been is rather unfriendly. In 1890 Edouard de Morsier included a lengthy essay on Raabe in his book on *Romanciers allemands contemporains*. Raabe, as always, was grateful and acknowledged it as a contribution to peaceful French-German relations, but privately he thought it rather naive (E 2: 285-86). A Grenoble dissertation by Selma Fliess on Raabe's life, early literary influences, and philosophy appeared in 1912; I have never seen it, and it has long been forgotten. There has been very little translation into French and none since 1931. Indeed, Kientz may be largely responsible for this lack of interest, for his book is dispiritingly refractory and in places even denunciatory. Here I can do no better than quote my earlier comment on it: Kientz

> takes a perversely negative view of Raabe as an undisciplined, disorderly person, full of the class-consciousness of bourgeois officialdom, shiftily seeking social standing as a writer. Kientz... invents traits and motives for which there is no evidence, is incapable of distinguishing voices in the text, and is sometimes very inaccurate. He seems mainly to deplore that Raabe was not a French realist of clearly focused rationalistic philosophy, and he is particularly bewildered by

Raabe's ambiguity, irony, and refusal to take clearly defined positions: "Raabe apparaît comme un esprit incapable de prendre nettement parti, de faire un choix net, de se construire une pensée réellement à lui." (Sammons 1987, 60, quoting Kientz 1939, 119)

Now one can see from this strange book that Kientz was an intelligent and sometimes observant critic. In fact, after World War II, in a survey of Raabe's reputation in foreign lands, the admirable Constantin Bauer even partly defended Kientz against the understandable antipathy to him in the Raabe community, asserting that, along with much that is false, his book contains "eine Fülle von treffenden Beobachtungen und feinsinnigen Bemerkungen" (Bauer 1956, 8). It would not be implausible to suppose that the affect pervading the book is national and political in origin, for by 1939 we are not only well into the Nazi period but even farther into the near-fatal perversion of Wilhelm Raabe into a precursor of fascism.

c: Crime and Punishment

When a forthright critique of the Raabe-Gesellschaft's Nazi complicities appeared in the very *Raabe-Jahrbuch* (Töteberg and Zander, 1973), one of the stalwarts, the loyal bibliographer Fritz Meyen (1902-74), attempted to mount a critique (the last contribution of his life, as it turned out). Among the points in this painfully shrill defense (from which the editorship of the *Jahrbuch* distanced itself in a postscript) is the assertion that the Raabe-Gesellschaft, like any other organization in Germany, was forced by the Nazi tyranny into compliance (Meyen 1974, 108). It is disagreeable to be obliged to say that this is not true and falsifies the long and often enthusiastic journey of the society into Nazification. Here we are at the farthest remove from something like the Browning Society, which in its evolution as a refuge for the religiously addled and the effetely poetic did no serious harm, except perhaps for a time to Browning's reputation. With the history of the Raabe-Gesellschaft we are dealing with much grimmer and more catastrophic complicities.

Parenthetically, the *Mitteilungen* give us a glimpse from the inside into one of the disasters that made Germans long for radical salvation. From the outset membership in the Raabe-Gesellschaft had been five marks a quarter, a figure intended to be low enough to exclude no interested person on the grounds of means. In the course of 1922 it began to rise, accompanied by apologies and worries about financial difficulties. In early 1923 the dues went to eighty marks a quarter; an appeal for funds had raised 280,000 marks, but this endowment was already being eroded. In the second quarter the dues were one hundred marks, in the third five hundred, in the fourth thirty million (or twenty gold pfennigs). A professor in Illinois sent 1,234,000 marks, but to no avail. As happened to many organizations and to individuals as well, a bank cancelled the society's account because the seven-million-mark balance was too small to maintain. Finally in 1924 the dueş were fixed at two gold marks (*Mitt.* 12 [1922]; 13 [1923]; 14 [1924]). It does not take much imagination to sense how destabilizing such an experience must be to one's fundamental personal and social being. However, it does not excuse or even explain the conduct of the Raabe-Gesellschaft, the roots of which long antedated the inflation.

A number of proto-fascist themes become common coin of the "friends'" discourse at a fairly early date. One of them is resentment at the lost war. This brings with it a degree of hostility to America, which we have already seen, and to England. Thus Wilhelm Stapel, in a contribution to the *Gedenkbuch* in 1921, speaks of the superiority of "die tiefe, tumbe deutsche Seele" over the "angelsächsisches ... Wesen." Associated with this line are attacks on Woodrow Wilson: "Wer keine Ohren hat, es [Raabe's message] zu hören, kann Stadtbaurat in Nippendorf und Präsident der Vereinigten Staaten von Nordamerika werden" (Bauer and Schultz 1921, 96, 99). One curious example of this is provided by Emil Doernenburg, a German-American who wrote a master's thesis on Raabe and Dickens at the University of Pennsylvania in 1908, which was published as a book in 1921 after having been revised by Wilhelm Fehse, and a doctoral dissertation, also at Pennsylvania, in 1913 on Raabe and Romanticism, published in 1919, and who strove to make Raabe known in America. He published an odd article in the *Mitteilungen* in 1913. He begins by saying the Germans have a false and shallow view of America and speaks of its achievements, which — and here he begins to fall into the enduring German clichés — have left it no time for culture, for making money is the beginning and end of American life. The best of Raabe is inaccessible to Americans, and the mass of them are not mature enough for him. But he places hopes in an awakening German-American community, for: "Die Edelsten der Welt sind aus deutschem Holze geschnitzt, welcher Nation sie auch immer angehören mögen" (Bauer 1925, 72-83). There is a certain poignancy in this nonsense, published just before World War I destroyed the prestige of the German-American community, for all practical purposes, forever. Bauer was later to say that Doernenburg had never felt at home in America and his every letter was full of forlorn longing for Germany (Bauer 1956, 6).

The scorn of the Weimar Republic, also already noted, is another recurrent theme. In an essay of 1922 on "Goethe, Raabe und die deutsche Zukunft," Fehse, claiming the German people are at a crossroads and need to find their way to the "heilige Quellen unserer deutschen Wesensart" and opposing "der deutsche Mensch in seiner Ursprünglichkeit, seiner lachenden Unbefangenheit" to "allen Mächten, die der Persönlichkeit Fesseln anlegen wollen," observes contemptuously that even "die Führer unseres republikanischen Deutschlands" could not avoid honoring Goethe (Fehse 1922, 12-14, 25). Racism and anti-Semitism establish themselves early also. In 1924 Fehse praised Raabe's race-consciousness, remarking of the noble and courageous Jewish heroine of *Frau Salome* that she was an exception, moved out of the "Schicksalsring ihres Rassentums" (Fehse 1924, 55-57). In 1927 an article appeared on "Wilhelm Raabe und die nordische Rasse" (Mohr 1927), a theme easily continued in the Nazi period (Hahne 1934). Consistent with these views is the anti-modern affect against civilization. In 1931, in one of the recurrent inquiries about Raabe's relevance to young people, one representative of them intones: "Mit ihm kämpfen wir gegen die moderne Zivilisation, die das Höchste und Heiligste sowohl im Menschen, als auch in der Gemeinschaft vernichtet" (Hertel 1931, 60). The disgust at Thomas Mann, noted above, is another motif that continues unabated into the Nazi period. Directly on the heels of the Nazi takeover Franz Hahne calls Mann "kein deutscher Dichter" because he was a foreigner owing to his "kreolschen Halbblut"; *Der Zauberberg* is not national but international (Hahne 1933b, 105). Hahne (1865-1955), a schoolteacher, a zealous Nazi, and a race-theory hobbyist, became president in 1932; with that act the Raabe-Gesellschaft

Nazified itself well before the regime "co-ordinated" it. Hahne supplied the preface to a monograph that, although it purports to deal with narrative technique, spends most of its time explicating Raabe's message of wisdom in traditional terms (Schneider 1936).

The record in the *Mitteilungen* is extensive and horrendous. Immediately upon Hitler's accession to power, Fehse addressed a sonnet to him (*Mitt.* 23 [1933]: 73), and in 1939, in support of German aggression against Czechoslovakia, printed another poem attacking the Czechs and Woodrow Wilson (*Mitt.* 29 [1939]: 1-3). In that same year, for Hitler's birthday, Hahne had a Hitler Youth prepare a calligraphic manuscript of *Des Reiches Krone,* and proudly printed Hitler's (or his staff's) two-line telegram of thanks (33-35); in the first issue of the following year Hahne sent Hitler congratulations for having survived the assassination attempt in the Bürgerbräukeller (*Mitt.* 30 [1940]: 1). Hahne and Fehse contributed articles portraying Raabe as a forerunner of Nazism, and another member of long standing compared Raabe and Hitler as religious thinkers (*Mitt.* 23 [1933]: 67-69; 24 [1934]: 1-8, 8-17). Anti-Semitic dicta abounded. As the war turned against Germany, the tone of the *Mitteilungen* became increasingly shrill and divorced from reality. It is a question whether we should be giving this episode any space at all; whether it is not irrelevant to a history of criticism. It is, however, a fateful moment in the history of Raabe's reputation, and it directly affects the history of criticism in two particular ways.

Needless to say, upon the official Nazification of the society, the Jewish members were expelled from the membership. The only member of prominence to protest was Constantin Bauer, who resigned the editorship of the *Mitteilungen,* a post he had held since 1912 (*Mitt.* 23 [1933]: 66). However, the whole situation may have quietly offended a good many other people; Horst Denkler reports that by 1935 the membership had shrunk by more than half (Denkler 1987a, 22). The most prominent victim of the expulsion was the literary historian Heinrich Spiero (1876-1947), who had known Raabe since 1901, had been one of the most faithful members of the society from the beginning, and had become its vice-president as well as for many years president of the Berlin chapter. He published the first general biography of Raabe in 1924, a lexicon of Raabe's sometimes exotic vocabulary in 1927, and the centenary volume in 1931 mentioned above. Spiero was Jewish only by racist definition; by religious affiliation he was a committed, active Protestant. But, like the others of Jewish origin, he was unceremoniously informed by a bank that he was no longer a member. Just how Spiero survived the Holocaust has never been told. Perhaps his church connections and the indulgence sometimes shown by Christians to baptized Jews will turn out to be the explanation; he himself ran an organization for the protection of non-Aryan Christians until it was banned in 1937, and later helped Jews in other ways. No one seemed grieved about his fate after the war. The Raabe-Gesellschaft tacitly readmitted him by including an article in the *Wilhelm Raabe-Kalender 1947* (Spiero 1946); in the list of contributors to the volume his first name is given as "Wilhelm." Upon his death the *Mitteilungen* carried a bland notice (*Mitt.* 35 [1948]: 36). Nothing much was done about him until Horst Denkler began to press for his rehabilitation, badgering the Berlin Senate to grant funds for a memorial on his grave, which the local chapter was finally able to acknowledge in 1990 (*Mitt.* 77 [1990]: 24).

Our sympathy for the pathos of Spiero's fate and our gratification at his rehabilitation, belated as it may be, should not obscure the recognition that he was a mediocre scholar and critic. None of his prolific writing, including his history of the German novel, published posthumously in 1950, is of much value today. He was an almost classical disciple: conservative, nationalistic, faithful to the values of the cult, conformist, and unimaginative. Some of his gestures of assimilation exceed the bounds of reason. In an article on Raabe's place in literary history he praised not only the nationalist and anti-Semitic historian Treitschke and the dubious Freytag, but also Adolf Bartels, a hysterical and vulgar anti-Semite who poured forth publications designed to eradicate the memory of Heinrich Heine from German culture (Bauer and Schultz 1921, 42-43). (An unsigned condemnation of Bartels's racist and nationalist excesses appeared in *Mitt.* 75 [1988]: 24-25, without mentioning that he was at one time a member of Raabe's entourage.) In every respect except for his expulsion Spiero is a typical and, indeed, central figure in the degradation and falsification of Raabe in the interwar years. His fate is sad to contemplate, but not tragic.

The other problem that bears upon the critical history is the enduring prominence in it of Wilhelm Fehse (1880-1946), who first makes an appearance in Raabe's diary at the age of nineteen or twenty in February 1900 and developed into what may have been the best mind the Raabe-Gesellschaft of that generation produced. Perhaps he seems so to the likes of me because he appears as the most scholarly in the conventional sense. He wrote much in the cultic spirit that is eminently forgettable, but beyond that he evidently set himself to be Raabe's definitive biographer. Along the way he produced a book on the longest-lived friendship in Raabe's life, with Wilhelm Jensen (Fehse 1940b), an edition of the letters (*"In alls gedultig"*) that, for reasons to be explained later, must still be employed today, and two full biographies (Fehse 1928, 1937). The second of these, which is, as far as I can see, the longest book ever written on Raabe, was, and is, the standard biography, having never been superseded, at least in its traditional, perhaps old-fashioned "life and works" form. And this is a misfortune, for the work, as one might expect from its date and from Fehse's record generally, is pervasively Nazified.

One can see the hardening of the position from the first version to the second. To be sure, there is a good deal of continuity. There is the same nationalistic and *völkisch* rhetoric. The anti-critical and anti-aesthetic position is similar. In 1928 Fehse calls Raabe "der deutsche Seher und Führer zum Leben," a vocation more important than that of the great artist (Fehse 1928, 9), and concludes by praising the "Raabemenschen": "Was ist ihnen Literatur! Sie blicken durch sie hindurch und suchen, was hinter ihr steht, erschütternd und erhebend zugleich" (314). In 1937 we find on the last page:

> Aber Raabe selbst hat seine *künstlerische* Sendung niemals für seine bedeutsamste gehalten. Unheimlich früh entsagte er dem Ehrgeiz einer rein literarischen Geltung. Ein schlichter, herzenswarmer Helfer und Tröster im Lebenskampf zu sein, erschien ihm ein schönerer Beruf. (Fehse 1937, 644)

In both works Stopfkuchen is identified with Raabe as a portrait of his personality and career (Fehse 1928, 274; 1937, 522-25).

Other positions, however, have changed, some subtly, some more noticeably, for example, in regard to *Stopfkuchen*. In 1928

Stopfkuchen's enemies represent "die Kanaille in uns" (Fehse 1928, 279), an observation that suggests at least a limited understanding of the way the narrative device works in that novel; by 1937 this sense of moral complicity has disappeared. Furthermore, there are signs of a certain depoliticization. In 1928 Fehse speaks of Raabe's resistance to Metternich and his system, and of his depiction of the police state at the time of the *Chronik* (33-34, 44); in 1937 these points are not stressed; rather the *Chronik* is more historicized, as protest against the aristocratic class (Fehse 1937, 67-76). In the earlier version one of the objects of the satire in *Eulenpfingsten* is said to be: "Die unausrottbare deutsche Unart, den politischen Gegner moralisch zu verfehmen" (Fehse 1928, 211); nothing more is said about this in 1937. In 1928 Fehse rather surprisingly speaks of the necessity of Naturalism, based on Socialism, in clearing the cultural air, despite its excesses (60), a comment that would not be thinkable in 1937.

In matters more essential to Nazi doctrine the differences are more evident. In 1928 Fehse expresses skepticism about the explanatory power of the "scientific" view of determination by race (12). By 1937 we are shown how there falls

> von Raabes Herkunft und von seiner rassischen Bedingtheit aus ein überraschend klärendes Licht nicht nur auf den Gehalt seines Werkes, sondern auch auf seine so oft mißverstandene und angefeindete Ausdrucksform, (Fehse 1937, 36)

and today we see how Raabe's anti-materialist humor exhibits "seine nahe Verwandtschaft mit dem Weltgefühl des nordischen Menschen" (642). Although the earlier book is sufficiently anti-Semitic, the later one is more systematic. In 1928, in identifying Raabe (against his will, incidentally), with *Heimatkunst,* Fehse mentions among the models the Jewish regionalist Berthold Auerbach (Fehse 1928, 40); in 1937 Auerbach is nowhere to be seen. Although, in the original treatment of *Der Hungerpastor,* Moses Freudenstein is illegitimately equated with Heine, Fehse speaks of Heine and Börne as renegade Jews, thus still reflecting, if imperfectly, the defense of Raabe and his apologists that Freudenstein, as a renegade, was not to be regarded as a typological Jewish character (38-39). When this topic is discussed in 1937, the ascription of anti-Semitic typology is much more assertive (Fehse 1937, 221). In 1928 Fehse speculated that the original plan of *Keltische Knochen* might have been an imitation of the tone of Heine's *Harzreise* (Fehse 1928, 139); nothing remains of this suggestion in 1937, where Fehse speaks instead of the influence of Jean Paul on the novella (Fehse 1937, 234). Concerning Frau Salome, Fehse in 1928 remarks cautiously: "die Rassenzuge-hörigkeit wird nicht übergangen" (Fehse 1928, 212), but he remembers that the "ichor," the fluid of the gods, flows in her blood as in that of all the positive characters. By 1937 Frau Salome is a pathetic figure who feels contempt for the race that shackles her (Fehse 1937, 405). Here, as elsewhere, Fehse makes as little as possible of Raabe's sympathetically drawn Jews. In his plot sum-mary of *Frau Salome* the title figure's role is considerably reduced; in the very brief account of *Höxter und Corvey*, the Jews, innocent scapegoats of all the contending parties, are barely mentioned, and the main Jewish figures not at all; instead Fehse links the story to contemporaneous events in French-German relations (399-401). Raabe now is finally vindicated as a national prophet:

> Der Glaube, daß die Zeit heute herangereift ist, an die Raabe in seinen deutschen Träumen gedacht hat, ist der Lebens-kern dieses Buches, (15),

at a time when

> Goethes Anschauung von einer organisch gebundenen, rassisch beseelten Volkheit ... den Sieg gewonnen über die blutleeren Wahngebilde eines wurzellosen Rationalismus [hat]. (643)

When this dream, perversely imputed to Raabe, exposed itself as a nightmare, retribution was harsh. In 1944 his granddaughter described the destruction of his apartment and its contents in Braunschweig in a British bombing raid (*Mitt.* 34, No. 2 [1944]: 43-45); earlier that year it had been reported that his grandson had been killed in Russia (*Mitt.* 34, No. 1 [1944]: 45-47). The *Mitteilungen* suspended publication in that year. Hahne was incapacitated in a bombing raid; a Braunschweig professor of medieval history, Ernst-August Roloff (1886-1955), under the "Führer principle" was appointed, not elected, to succeed him. Hahne died in 1955 at the age of ninety; the year before he had left the organization he had served so long in protest against a Raabe edition planned to appear in East Germany as well as in the west (*Mitt.* 42 [1955]: 108, 29). Fritz Jensch died in the fire-bombing of Hamburg, and Fehse in a Soviet detention camp; I have been told that he starved to death. The outcome was deplorable, but it is hard to be sympathetic.

Meanwhile, we are left with Fehse's biography of 1937. It was the only one in its time to benefit from access to the private papers of Raabe and his family. Unlike the earlier version, it has reference notes and an index. Although there has been important biographical writing in our time, as we shall see, nothing as thorough as Fehse's has been attempted since. In its bulk it symbolizes the obstacle that Raabe's modern reputation has had to surmount.

3: Rehabilitation

THE DECADE AND A HALF following upon the end of World War II constituted the lowest point in the history of Raabe's reputation from the time he first began publishing a hundred years before. I have noted in a couple of places that I cannot clearly recall his name so much as having been mentioned during my student years, even though my studies were already largely focused on the nineteenth century. My *Doktorvater* Heinrich Henel did not like him, and I have the feeling that this was true of many Germans of that era who were intensely anti-Nazi as Henel was. If so, this would be a clear symptom of the damage done to him by his "friends" in the interwar era.

The "friends," to be sure, now under the continued leadership of Roloff, made every effort to regroup in the midst of the ruins. The *Mitteilungen,* having given up with the 1944 issue, began to publish again in 1948. Roloff put out a *Raabe-Kalender* for 1947 and 1948, like its predecessor interspersing nuggets of Raabean wisdom with short articles, mostly biographical items or source studies. This populist form has a curiously anachronistic look to it, and it did not thrive. Roloff then tried with a *Raabe-Jahrbuch,* which again continued for only two years, 1949 and 1950. It did not differ much from the *Kalender,* except that it did not contain a calendar. For the next ten years the *Mitteilungen* remained the main organ of discourse about Raabe. What is so exasperating in retrospect about this period is the unwillingness or inability to come to terms with what had happened. In general this may seem as just one more symptom of the much-critized West German inclination to reconnect with the *status quo ante* and veil the Thousand-Year Reich in as much willful amnesia as could be mustered. In the case of Raabe, however, it must have required an unusual degree of blindness not to see that he could not be rescued in this manner.

a: From Quiescence to Recovery

The obfuscating gestures are too common and consistent to be totally sonambulistic. In the *Kalender* for 1947 Paul Fuchtel, now the editor of the *Mitteilungen*, contributed a four-page history of the *Raabe-Gesellschaft*. The recent past is got over as tersely as possible, with the first appearance of the myth that the society had been forced into collaboration. Fuchtel praises the, one would think, by now incriminated Hahne for having preserved the society through difficult times (Fuchtel 1946, 148). Hahne was, in fact, made honorary president (*Mitt.* 35 [1948]: 37); he published one more essay in Roloff's short-lived *Jahrbuch* (Hahne 1950); and in a retrospect Roloff's son (who wrote his dissertation on *Prinzessin Fisch*) praised his leadership again and even hinted at a resistance legend (Roloff [Jun.], 1951a). The first, brief allusion to the evils of the Nazi period in the *Mitteilungen* appeared in 1951 and came from a member in New York (Buchholz 1951). In 1957 Hans Oppermann, about whom more shortly, published an encomium on Fehse, not mentioning such things as the sonnet to Hitler (Oppermann 1957). Some things genuinely bizarre in their insensitivity occurred in this period. In 1949 the Dessau chapter, in a catch-up report on its doings since the suspension of the *Mitteilungen*, recorded with a straight face a lecture by Colin Ross in 1943 on American propaganda (*Mitt.* 36 [1949]). Ross, one of the more crackpot ideologues of the Nazi movement, had prophesied the takeover and purification of America by its superior German element in two books published in 1936, *Unser Amerika* and *Amerikas Schicksalsstunde*. Finally in 1951, Bauer, who may appear as the one genuine "Raabemensch" in this milieu, in an issue celebrating the fortieth anniversary of the society, reproved its sentimentality, lack of scholarly outlook, and refusal of criticism, in his opinion, out of concern for the Raabe family (Bauer 1951), and in 1956 he commented on the Nazi treatment of Raabe in the *Mitteilungen,* for which he gave chapter and verse, as a burden on the author's reputation in foreign lands (Bauer 1956, 10).

An occasional dissertation emerged during this period. A quite brief one in Munich by Thea Heinrich dealt with the topic of death in Raabe's works. This is indeed a pertinent topic, though Heinrich's existentialist, philosophical approach still bears the earmarks of employing Raabe as a source of wisdom and consolation. The dissertation was directed by Hans Heinrich Borchert. This is interesting, for Borchert had directed a dissertation, published in 1942, entitled *Das Ich als Schicksal und Aufgabe in den Dichtungen Raabes* by Günther Vogelsang, who fell in Russia before receiving his degree. It is a turgidly idealistic, existentialist exercise that I, at any rate, found virtually unreadable. In a preface Borchert praises Vogelsang for having been an early and enthusiastic Nazi (Vogelsang 1942, 3). Heinrich explicitly refers to Vogelsang as a model (Heinrich 1949, 21). In all this we see another one of the disturbing lines of continuity in academia between the Third Reich and the Federal Republic. In the following year a Bonn dissertation, also on death, by Christel Schmitz appeared. It is of little value; it treats Raabe's works as a unified body of homiletic texts, showing the harmony of life and death and death's relative unimportance. We are told that true "Raabemenschen" show a readiness for death and a belief in fate, but we also learn from the master gratitude for life: "Dieser Dank dem gelebten Leben gegenüber ist das Vermächtnis Raabes an unsere Zeit, sein Ruf aus der Vergangenheit an jede künftige Gegenwart" (Schmitz 1950, 66, 63). That this fustian could be accepted as a doctoral dissertation just a few years after the orgies of death among the Germans and their victims is a depressing sign of some aspects of those times. More of a curiosity is Maria Vogel's 1949 medical dissertation from Frankfurt on psychic abnormalities of Raabe's characters and their psychiatric interpretation. The author identifies seventy psychotics in Raabe's works and endeavors to attach a clinical label to each (Vogel 1949). One is tempted to believe that this is the product of a young woman in a hurry to become a physician in difficult times.

There were, however, a few stronger dissertations. One from Bonn in 1953 by Aloise Esser treats structure in Raabe's historical novellas. In eight texts she analyzes levels of historical time and the relationship of narrative and narrated time. She has a particularly good section on *Höxter und Corvey*, which, she points out, has the longest narrative time but the shortest narrated time of all the eight, but the same time period is depicted in several strands from different perspectives (Esser 1953, 78-82). This technical analysis is a clear sign that the literary criticism of Raabe is beginning to come of age in the 1950s. However, what was probably the most enduringly valuable dissertation of that decade was never published: Karl Heim's inquiry into Raabe's relationship with his public (Heim 1953). This truly absorbing study from Tübingen was well ahead of its time in the attention it gave to the economic and sociological context of a writer's career. Raabe's often tense relations with his twenty-two publishers, his struggles with intrusive editors, misery at having to meet the requirements of magazine serialization, frustration at the indifference of the public, and inability to recognize with a whole heart popularity and prosperity when it came to him late in his career, along with many other useful details, are solidly and intelligently treated. Perhaps it is a sign of the still lurking inhibitions of the Raabeans that, while a number of indifferent dissertations from these years, including some not mentioned here, were printed, Heim's reposes as a faded, barely legible copy in the Braunschweig archive, of which only a brief abstract appeared in the *Mitteilungen* (Heim 1955). Even after nearly forty years it might still be usefully published.

Constituting more of a link with the past is Siegfried Hajek's book, *Der Mensch und die Welt im Werk Wilhelm Raabes* of 1950. The view of Raabe is still old-fashioned and, as it seems to me, too religious, and he is still presented a resource of comfort in troubled times. Hajek's discussions of individual texts can be intelligent, but sometimes suffer from a need to find harmonious, peaceful messages. Thus he interprets Phöbe in *Unruhige Gäste* as an undeveloped child and the retarded Ludchen Bock in *Altershausen* as superior to the mature Feyerabend, positions that I do not believe can be sustained. Disruptive aspects of texts, such as the dreams in *Altershausen*, tend to be ignored. However, even here the focus on individual texts is sharper and more detailed than had been the custom, showing that a judicious spirit is beginning to enter the discourse.

Perhaps the most remarkable event in this period was the appearance in 1958 of a full-scale life and works by Hermann Pongs (b. 1889), another disturbing case of the survival of an academic reputation from the Third Reich into the Federal Republic. In the *Mitteilungen* of 1933 that enthusiastically greeted the Nazi accession to power Pongs was promptly at hand with an article on "Raabe und das Reich," where we hear of him "als Prediger vom Wesen des Deutschen Menschen und vom Reich der Deutschen im geschichtlichen und ewigen Sinn" (Pongs 1933, 5). This is actually a lecture that he had given before the Nazi coup, in November 1932, and he defends himself against a charge in the press that he meant to make Raabe "den Dichter des 'dritten Reiches'" (13). Perhaps Pongs should be regarded as more radically conservative than fascist, as when he asserts: "Der Mensch Raabes ... ist der wahrhaft konservative Mensch als *der gebundene Mensch*, gebunden in den geschichtliche und ewigen Zusammenhang" (12), but when he expresses his allegiance to the likes of Möller van den Bruck and Hanns Johst the distinction becomes harder to discern. In the midst of the catastrophic circumstances of 1944 Pongs found time to contribute an essay on "Frauenehre bei Raabe," full of Nordic honor, tribal values, and Germanic archetypes. His most entertaining passage asserts that in Helene in *Die Akten des Vogelsangs*

> hat Raabe hier bereits den amerikanischen Typus Frau vorgebildet, wie ihn der moderne amerikanische Roman herausarbeitet: an allen Seelenkräften verdorrt, eitel, lebensgierig, grausam, leer. (Pongs 1944, 14-15)

Pongs's book, which both in its bulk and an occasional aside indicates a desire to compete with if not to displace Fehse's biography, exhibits a certain tension between old habits and adaptations to the changed environment. Familiar are the values of unity, harmony, equilibrium, underlying religiousness, and the spirit of order. Pongs retains the subordination of artistry, in this case to a symbolizing instinct, and insists that Raabe is to be interpreted from "Gemüt," not from his context (Pongs 1958, 7). Raabe's ideal is anti-Faustian, "den Menschen im Zusammenhang der Dinge ... er will nicht den Unmenschen oder Übermenschen, sondern den Mitmenschen" (14). It was Brandes who understood him best, with "Gemüt" as the center; his characteristics to be stressed are mysticism, simplicity, humbleness, and childlikeness (633). How much better is the simplicity and "Lebenshilfe" of *Das Horn von Wanza* than the comic realism of Gogol! (473). Echoing the line of argument in his 1944 paper, he proclaims of Helene: "Die Verkletterung in den amerikanischem Mammonismus wird zum repräsentativen Zeitsymptom" (608). He comments on Raabe's Lower Saxon tribal identity (52). He attacks Thomas Mann and argues that Raabe parodied Ibsen (23-27, 607). He praises Adolf

Bartels, Josef Nadler, the Nazi literary historian Paul Fechter, and
the seriously compromised Franz Koch, but also — and here we see
the adaptability — the Canadian Barker Fairley and the English-
man Roy Pascal (32).

There are a number of more up-to-date gestures. Pongs several
times distances himself from Nazism. Heine is restored to Raabe's
pantheon (203). Moses Freudenstein in *Der Hungerpastor* is not a
typological Jew (219); the helpless Jews in *Höxter und Corvey* attract
the beastliness in man (345). Pongs is fair to Frau Salome (357, 361)
and cites approvingly the Jewish philosopher Hermann Cohen (362-
63). For the first time since the writings of Josef Bass forty years
before, the reader is reminded that Raabe explicitly refused to be
associated with anti-Semitism (416). Freud is invoked, if somewhat
lukewarmly (326, 621). Pongs has no compunctions about criticism;
in fact, he is eloquently disdainful of Raabe's early works. This
devaluation of the early works has become such a commonplace in
criticism that it may well be due for some revision, but at the time
of which we are speaking it was not customary. Pongs complains of
sentimentality, ostentatious allusiveness, triviality, and all but
meretriciousness. Even the *Chronik,* usually exempted from such
strictures, does not escape; Pongs finds Wachholder's wisdom
contradictory and confused (89). The evaluative rock bottom is in
Auf dunklem Grunde, which he characterizes as "Kitsch der Zeit"
and an "Ansammlung von Gemüts-Greueln" (151-52), whatever
they may be. Perhaps owing to its patriotic theme, he is less hard on
Nach dem großen Kriege, which I have always thought to be the
rock bottom, but even here he is cool (155-58). He finds *Die Leute
aus dem Walde* derivative of Goethe's *Wilhelm Meister* as well as
of Dickens and others (167-70). Even the middle works are not
highly praised. He disparages *Drei Federn* as lacking in true
symbolism (235); like older critics, he shows no interest in its
narrative innovation. He is uneasy at *Abu Telfan* as dishar-
monious (265), and, with a quite traditional view of Raabe's
"humor," he is not amused by the comic works, such as *Der
Dräumling,* in which he seems to find Schiller dishonored and
which shows not the naive folk but the blind mass (313, 317); and
of course not by the raucous *Christoph Pechlin,* which lacks the
freedom (by which is meant, the idealism) of the humorist (321).
He does not seem to find Raabe achieving excellence until 1877-78,

with *Alte Nester*. Of *Stopfkuchen* he asserts that it is the first of Raabe's works to reach the rank of the great novels of world literature (552); no traditional critic would have allowed himself the implied restrictiveness of this judgment. He implicitly ascribes to Raabe what under the Nazis would have been serious delinquency: cosmopolitanism; the common grave of German and French soldiers in *Kloster Lugau* Pongs interprets as "eine Warnung an die Völker Europas, nicht ihr bestes Blut gegenseitig zu verschleudern, das namenlose treue Volk" (587).

It is annoying, in these circumstances, to be obliged to recognize that Pongs, whatever his moral condition may have been, was a learned and intelligent scholar, and that there are insights of value in this oddly hybrid book. His unusual critique of the *Chronik* is by no means unreasonable. He is quite skeptical of a talk Raabe gave to the *Kleiderseller* on his fiftieth birthday in 1881 — one of his few published pieces of non-fiction — in which he seems to reinforce the notions of the typical, bourgeois, philistine "Raabemenschen" as a special people, humorous, modest, and indifferent to philistines. Pongs, who is much better at censuring than at celebrating, calls this performance "echt demokratische Stammtisch-Mystik" and claims that Raabe is wearing the "Maske des Stammtisch-Philisters" (410-11), something I have thought must be at least partly the case. A certain disturbance or indecisiveness that seems to mark his response to *Die Akten des Vogelsangs* is a plausible reaction to that elusive work. His explanation of the reason why Valerie at the end of *Unruhige Gäste* sends Phöbe an ancient Christian lamp as a gift, and why Phöbe interprets it as intended to humiliate her, is the only one I have encountered that makes sense to me (510; cf. Sammons 1987, 247). It would be nice to be tolerant and even-handed. But the history of our times makes it inappropriate in a case like that of Pongs. His book was not especially well received at the time, nor is it often cited today. A rather acid review essay on it pointed out that he seemed to have forgotten the use made of "Gemüt" and "Innerlichkeit" in the recent past (Weniger 1958, 614).

Another career shows that origins in the Nazi period need not necessarily burden or taint the work of a literary scholar of genuine ability and thoughtfulness: that of Fritz Martini. It began right at the outset of the Third Reich with a Berlin dissertation of 1933 by the twenty-four-year-old on spaces in Raabe's writing, published in part in the following year as *Die Stadt in der Dichtung Wilhelm Raabes*. Here we see an early phase of the task Martini set himself unremittingly into our time: the definition of realism in German literature. His views on this, and on Raabe's place within realism, change somewhat or shift their emphases over the years, as he become increasingly expert in the ambiguity and elusiveness of the problem. In the published dissertation he argues that in Raabe the self is determined by a reality that already has an immanent, material order, thus distinguishing him from the idealism of the "Poetic Realists" (Martini 1934b, 8). Martini says quite rightly that Raabe was "fanatisch bürgerlich" (38), yet recognizes at the same time that he was internally critical of the bourgeois order. Raabe is compared to Auerbach fairly without any anti-Semitic undertone (21-22), and Martini does not make him, as more conventional observers were inclined to do, implacably hostile to the city, although he rightly observes that Raabe was attached to a disappearing small town culture and that this is a Biedermeier feature of his work (42-44). When he sees Raabe as an enemy of modern civilization (34, 44), this may be a contamination from the ideological environment.

In the year before, Martini published an essay on Raabe and the nineteenth century that again shows him not uninfluenced by the environment but seeking his own perspective. Unconsciously echoing Perquin, Martini asserts that Raabe's fundamental motive is the question whether there is an ethical law located in and realized by life (Martini 1933b, 327). He traces the ambiguity of Raabe's relationship to his times between an apparently congenital pessimism and an optimism he imposed upon himself, though his resignation and accommodation to the times is less affirmative, as is Goethe's and Keller's, than flight from "Verneinung und Selbstzerstörung" (332, 339-40, 337). He remarks that Raabe was not a humorist, but basically tragic (341). Even when the vocabulary of the time slips in, it seems to be used cautiously. For example, he observes that Raabe was "nicht von imperialem, sondern von völkischem Denken getragen" (338). The distinction between "imperial" and "völkisch" has the effect of literalizing the latter term to a meaning something like "populist." To the first Nazified issue of the *Mitteilungen* in 1933 Martini contributed an article in which he stresses Raabe's distinctiveness from the Biedermeier.

While he endeavors to set Raabe in his literary context, especially in regard to Adalbert Stifter, he presents him as passing through the Biedermeier, leaving its cultural ideal behind (Martini 1933a, 35, 40-41, 45). It is primarily with this text in mind that the modern historian of the Raabe-Gesellschaft, Eugen Rüter, who is far from inclined to overlook disabling continuities from past to present, remarks that Martini had wholly undermined the "friends'" view of Raabe without their noticing it:

> Seine Charakterisierung des Biedermeiers als einer "zurück- und vorwärtsweisenden Entwicklungsstufe des bürgerlichen Denkens," die Raabe so entscheidend beeinflußt habe, nahm den gerade während der Erscheinungszeit des Beitrages (1933) so häufigen Versuchen, Raabe zum Verkünder völkischen Ideengut zu machen, jede Berechtigung. (Rüter 1977, 81)

In 1934 Martini published an essay on the peasant in Raabe, a topic that invites ideological complicity. But again it is handled in a balanced way. Again Raabe is compared fairly with Auerbach, who is praised as a model of substance whose mode was turned into kitsch by his imitators (Martini 1934a, 70). Raabe rejected the fashionable village tale and sought more accurate representation. He saw more of the tension and oppression in peasant life, and portrayed peasants' rigidity, especially in *Die Leute aus dem Walde, Horacker*, and *Unruhige Gäste* (73). The mention of *Horacker* points to an excellent essay Martini published on that text in 1968, stressing the originality of Raabe's narrative procedure, his display of fictionality, mixture of styles, and parodies of literary and social clichés, and concluding that for Raabe the depiction of the idyll was possible only with the integration of the language of irony (Martini 1968, 232-36, 245, 250-54, 265). In 1935 Martini published an article on the problem of German realism in connection with Raabe in *Dichtung und Volkstum*, the renamed *Euphorion*. He begins by blithely asserting that the realists are "besonders deutsch und stammhaft gebunden" (Martini 1935, 271). But almost immediately he goes on to express his worry that nationalist arguments blur distinctions "um einer völkisch-metaphysischen Ganzheit willen" (272); so much for that. He then goes on to argue, I think rightly, that Raabe is more of a typical realist than Keller since he incorporates the insoluble problematics of realism (274). He seeks to locate Raabe in a history of post-Romantic writing beginning with Jean Paul, arguing that he came to disbelieve in early realism's ideal of ethical-religious harmony, with the consequence that he despaired of the necessity of external reality, a threat of meaninglessness first articulated in *Abu Telfan*, until he reoriented himself on the higher synthesis of the late Goethe (283, 288), while retaining a tragic and bitter outlook. He observes that Raabe, again unlike Keller, saw death as a negation of reality: "Diese immer wieder angedeutete Gebrochenheit seines Weltbildes wird nur mühsam in der Resignation verdeckt" (300). The claim of an orientation on Goethe, a traditional device for upgrading a writer, along with other details of interpretation in this essay, cannot, I think, be sustained, and there are other slips into the jargon of the time. All the same, the article is another example of a young, vigorous mind at work on the Raabe problem.

All of this was a prelude to Martini's important role in the modern criticism of Raabe, his studies always turning again and again to the problem of realism. In 1953 he published an essay on *Höxter und Corvey*, in which he showed how its jagged, chaotic form, unappreciated in the past, was appropriate to the chaotic circumstances, and stressed the innocence of the persecuted Jews as scapegoats (Martini 1953). In 1959 he placed in a pedagogical magazine a fine analysis of *Prinzessin Fisch*; in it he provided an excellent explication of the meaning of the phrase: "Der Zusammenhang der Dinge," which recurs in Raabe and even more in the critical literature (reprinted Helmers 1968a, 171-72). In 1964 he wrote of the fragmentary *Altershausen* that for Raabe, unlike Stifter, age was not a time of harmony and wisdom, but of disquiet; he supposed that Raabe did intend a closure of the text, but not a harmonious or unambiguous one; he pointed out the almost literal ambiguity of the figure of Ludchen Bock and that Feyerabend's dreams yield truth and bitterness (Martini 1964). In 1981 he published a study of *Meister Autor*, which exhibited for the first time, I believe, an insight into the dubiousness and unease of the narrator and his tendency to trivialize the Master Author's experiences (Martini 1981); this led to a worthwhile, instructive debate with Siegfried Hajek, published in the following year (Hajek and Martini, 1982). Martini also contributed a useful general chapter on Raabe to Benno von Wiese's *Deutsche Dichter des 19.*

Jahrhunderts of 1969. Already here he shows himself quite within the modern phase of interpretation. He now defines the reality in Raabe's realism as dreamlike, illusionary, a theater (Martini 1969, 534). Raabe stands in a dialectical, ironic relationship to contemporary conventional forms (540). Concerning the narrative ingenuity Martini speaks of a bipolarity:

> Er löst im Abstand erinnernder Reflexion ein Spannungs-verhältnis zwischen dem Erzähler und der erzählten Welt aus, das sich kritisch, ironisch, oder in einer Mehrdeutigkeit äußert, die zwischen dem Erzählten und dem Gemeinten eine Distanz läßt, einen Spielraum öffnet, in dem sich der Humor ansiedelt. Die Schwierigkeit der adäquaten Raabe-Interpretation liegt darin, daß beide Pole oft zu einer darstellerisch-sprachlichen Simultanität ineinandergeschichtet werden — derart, daß Identifikation und Distanz, Emotion und Ironie, Ergriffenheit und Humor kaum von einander ablösbar erscheinen. (549)

Martini's development, his continuous process of learning and refinement, have carried us beyond the advent of the modern phase, so that we must go back somewhat to pick up its beginnings.

b: The Advent of Critical Maturity

In 1961 Hermann Pongs sent an article he had written to the presidents of all the Raabe-Gesellschaft chapters, urging them to rebel against the new *Raabe-Jahrbuch* on the grounds that it was destroying the traditional image, introducing an avant-garde spirit, and suppressing the master's "Grundwesen ..., das nun einmal starke konservative, in allen Herzenskräften gegründeten Welt-einsichten hat" (Schrader 1977, 179). That Pongs was in such distress is a sign that something of significance was taking place in Raabe criticism. The significant moment can with fair precision be dated in the year 1960, the fiftieth anniversary of Raabe's death. That was the first year of the *Jahrbuch der Raabe-Gesellschaft*, edited by Karl Hoppe (1892-1973), a professor at the Technical University of Braunschweig, who had first emerged in the *Mitteilungen* during the Nazi years (he was an officer in both world wars), but came to be an important bridging figure between the past and the future and was president of the Raabe-Gesellschaft from

1957 to 1971. The *Jahrbuch* (the 1962 volume of which constituted a Festschrift for Hoppe) established itself at once as the vehicle for scholarly study, while the still continuing *Mitteilungen* has reverted to the status of a newsletter, containing news of the society and its chapters, along with notes and queries and other miscellanea. In the same year the new standard edition, the "Braunschweiger Ausgabe," also under the general editorship of Hoppe, was taken over by the publishing house of Vandenhoeck & Ruprecht in Göttingen. It had begun in 1951 with Klemm in Berlin, an old publisher of Raabeana, but the Göttingen republication is the one now most commonly in circulation. It has reached twenty volumes of text with four supplementary volumes and, although it is not complete — another volume of non-fictional writings containing the second version of *Ein Frühling* and other paralipomena is yet to appear — second editions of some of the volumes began to come out in 1966. The apparatus to each text gives an account of its genesis and publication history, reception in those cases where there is any to speak of, variant readings, preceded by a section called "Textbefund und Textgestaltung" (a very detailed account of Raabe's usage and diction that cannot be of much interest to many users), and annotation.

It was an ambitious and courageous undertaking at a time when Raabe's reputation had by no means fully recovered. It has, however, been subjected to a considerable amount of criticism. The volume editors vary in ability; especially Pongs was an egregiously poor choice as editor of *Der Hungerpastor* (vol. 6), with the consequence that, in contrast to the usual practice of the edition, practically nothing is said there of the important and disturbing reception history of the novel. Despite the detail of the apparatus, there have been complaints that it is not thorough or consistent, and that the texts themselves are hybrid (see Goldammer 1988). This is a consequence of the fact that Raabe, while reading proof of new editions, sometimes made adjustments and corrections, while overlooking earlier errors and editor's changes, and at the same time new misprints would be generated by subsequent printings. The edition, instead of identifying, as is customary in variorum editing, one text as the base, has tried to select from the variants what seems to be the best reading, thus in many cases generating an entirely new text that never existed before. One of the volume editors, Hans Butzmann, tried to protest against this and other editorial vagaries in the *Mitteilungen* as early as 1955, but Hoppe suppressed his article (Dittrich 1984). In recent years several of the texts have been reedited in paperback series such as Reclam and Deutscher Taschenbuch Verlag. To what extent these mostly microphilological problems affect interpretation is hard to say. For the more general user like myself the most disappointing aspect of the edition is its letter volumes. The second supplementary volume contains a selection of Raabe's letters, without those addressed to him. Since it does not include all those published by Fehse in his volume of correspondence of 1940 under the authentic but nevertheless tendentious title of *"In alls gedultig,"* we are not yet liberated from Fehse in this area; furthermore, many other scattered letters have been published at intervals in the *Mitteilungen* and the *Jahrbuch*. The annotation is skimpy and frustrating to use. The third supplementary volume is at least a complete correspondence, that of Raabe (and his wife) with Wilhelm and Marie Jensen. Here the annotation is somewhat better, but the lack of an index is an added frustration. It is now recognized that new edition of correspondence is one of the desiderata of Raabe scholarship (Denkler 1987a, 23; also 1988a, 152).

In the first issue of the *Jahrbuch* in 1960 Hoppe placed an edition of Raabe's aphorisms (Hoppe 1960a, 94-139). These sayings had long been part of the wisdom literature of the Raabe cult, but Hoppe was the first to edit them in chronological order. Many of them are indeed interesting, but it is necessary to be a little careful with them, for one never knows their purpose. Given Raabe's propensity to speak in multiple voices, they might as easily be intended as utterances of one fictional character or another as of Raabe's true self. Also in what begins to appear as an *annus mirabilis*, Hoppe published a selected volume of Raabe's drawings (Hoppe 1960b). One or another of these informal but undoubtedly talented and oddly telling sketches had also been known to the afficionados, but it has been a pleasure for the connoisseurs to have over a hundred of them clearly and generously reproduced with an instructive commentary. The drawings have drawn attention elsewhere. Herbert Senk, who mounted an exhibit of them in the muncipal museum of Braunschweig in 1954, wrote three thoughtful articles about their evolution and stylistic characteristics, the third of which attempts to link their strong black-and-white contrasts with

Raabe's writing style (Senk 1954, 1955, 1956). Another selection appeared in 1983, though with a commentary that is very dependent upon Hoppe's (Peter 1983). A highly professional consideration of them was presented to the Berlin Raabe conference of 1987 (Arndt 1988).

Hoppe also influenced scholarship. One of his protégés was Gerhart Mayer, who wrote under Hoppe's direction a *Habilitationsschrift* on Raabe's relationship to philosophy. This has always been a somewhat difficult topic, for Raabe shows little overt interest in philosophy, and no systematic interest at all. This presents a problem for German critics, who often believe that writers cannot create without the help of philosophers or look upon literature as philosophical discourse in different clothing. Furthermore, Raabe had a great many interests and was a constant and wide reader, so that he certainly was in touch with philosophical matters. His admirers have recurrently endeavored to link him more closely with them, especially his "pessimism" with the philosophy of Schopenhauer. He himself played his usual game of hide-and-seek with this matter. Repeatedly he denied Schopenhauer's influence on him; he really did not like to be thought of as having been influenced by anyone. On the other hand, he also acknowledges Schopenhauer, echoes or quotes him in several places, gives him a cameo role in *Eulenpfingsten*, and, as we can see from his diary and the books in his library, studied him with some attention. A Netherlandic scholar, Th. C. van Stockum, tried to cope with the problem by examining a single work, *Meister Autor*. He argues that the text exhibits a view of life as, on the whole, a bad experience, but that Raabe was less metaphysical than Schopenhauer, less grim and aggressive, and less committed to pessimism (Stockum 1921, 174, 182-83). In 1938 Reinhold Weinhardt took up the matter again. His study is useful in that it works out the exact chronology of Raabe's interest in the philosopher and calls attention to the genuine echoes and responses. But Weinhardt is such an enthusiastic disciple of Schopenhauer, at the expense of Nietzsche, that after a while the article looks like an effort to enroll Raabe in his club.

Mayer proceeds more expansively, attempting to pursue any possible philosophical influence, including that of Hegelianism in Berlin, Jacob Böhme at one stage, and stoicism at another, though he, too, comes to discuss Schopenhauer extensively. In distin-guishing the writer from the philosopher, he makes the excellent point that for Raabe the meaning of the world was not absent but *hidden;* thus his "pessimism" was not systematic (Mayer 1960, 46). He describes Raabe in his final period as breaking with stoicism and coming to an affirmation of life through humor. The mobilization of humor as a source of resolution still has an old-fashioned ring to it, though Mayer does insist that Raabe's comic aspect must also be considered together with the humor (60), a connection that older critics were unwilling to make. There are other old-fashioned features, especially a recourse to Goethe as a model of equilibrium, leading to what I believe is an excessively harmonious interpreta-tion of *Altershausen* (75). But Mayer sees Raabe in his third period parodying Schopenhauer in *Wunnigel* and struggling with nihil-istic implications in *Die Akten des Vogelsangs,* and ultimately he is not sure that humor has been the cure:

> Mochte Raabe auch unter dem Vorzeichen eines behaglich-weltverachtenden Humors wieder festen Boden gewonnen haben, so schloß das doch nicht den steten Zweifel an der Richtigkeit und Dauerhaftigkeit dieser Lösung aus. (84)

Meyer's monograph, which contains a number of local observa-tions worth considering, has the status of one of the standard works about Raabe's thought.

An unpublished Heidelberg dissertation of 1960 by Christa Hebbel also moves into the new era by analyzing narrative and figural perspectives in first-person narrations; as in the case of Heim, one must wonder why one of the more original and useful dissertations remained unpublished. Hebbel interestingly associates the doubleness in the narrative voice with a constant tension between humane values and the automatism of an amoral, value-free life process (Hebbel 1960, 6). Raabe's habit of presenting events and experiences through their reflexivity in consciousness has the effect of dissolving the "real" or "pragmatic" nexus (123), and direct dialogue functions this way also: it does not lead to greater realism but to "eine reflexive und zugleich subjektive Distanzierung vom rein Ereignismäßigen" (127). Hebbel's observations on individual works are always worth considering even if we may not agree with them, and she is constantly concerned to show that Raabe's texts do not provide unified messages or resolutions. Even of one of his most positive characters, Just Everstein in *Alte Nester*, she writes that his position does not have absolute validity but is illuminated and limited by other viewpoints (147). Hebbel genuinely breaks with the image of Raabe as guru dispensing consolation and guidance by stressing the persistently shifting ground:

> Wir würden es als die Eigentümlichkeit der Dichtung Raabes bezeichnen, daß in ihr weder die Überwindung aller Spannungen in der Tiefe des Gemüts noch die Ambivalenz des Sehens absolute Gültigkeit besitzt. (230)

Another dissertation, written in Göttingen in 1958 and published in 1960, was to open a career that was unfortunately cut short but was to be of signal importance in the development of modern Raabe criticism: that of Hermann Helmers (1923-87). His study of the "bildende Mächte" is actually an interpretive examination of the "Stuttgart trilogy" and the "Braunschweig trilogy." As far as *Bildung* is concerned, relatively little is effected from the customary sources, family and educational institutions. In all the cases the families are damaged and incomplete (Helmers 1960, 19); later it is said that the second group shows more respect between the generations of parents and children (62), but this is certainly not true of *Stopfkuchen* and not to any great extent of *Alte Nester*. School is a weak and negative institution; the cultural canon is present by allusion and quotation but is ironically employed (31). The good society of Vienna in *Der Schüdderump* is a form of philistinism (36). In the second group Helmers, in contrast to earlier interpreters, differentiates between author and narrator (68). The narrators are learned but not wise; their assimilation to society blocks their critical view (91-92). Through many details Helmers means to highlight Raabe's socially critical dimension, his resistance to the bourgeoisie, to which he himself belongs, so that he does not spare himself (100-01). This view hardly seems revolutionary today, but at the time it was perceived as a programmatic reversal of received opinion.

Two years later, in an article on Raabe's language, Helmers analyzed the variants to chapter 4 of *Abu Telfan* to show how Raabe's stylistic idiosyncrasies were worked into the text, thus a product of artistic will and not simply hindrances to the "message" (Helmers 1962). In an article on "Verfremdung als epische

Grundtendenz" he argued that Raabe's mixture of styles, his mixed metaphors and rhetorical freaks, his apparently irrelevant allusions and shifts of perspective all served the purpose of cultural criticism and the exposure of dissonances (Helmers 1963). Helmers became the author of the Sammlung Metzler volume on Raabe in 1968 (second edition, 1978). It is in the nature of the eminently useful Metzler volumes that they endeavor to supply fundamental information and bibliography at an introductory level; even here, however, Helmers stresses that the Raabe of 1968 is a new Raabe, but it is not he who has changed; it is the past that has failed to understand him (Helmers 1968b, v), and the last section is entitled "Gesellschafts- und Kulturkritik" (79-81). In that same year, at a time when new views were vociferously demanded in German literary studies, Helmers edited what was widely seen as a landmark volume, *Raabe in neuer Sicht*.

There is not space here to discuss the full importance of this collection of past and recent studies. Some of them — Lukács's overall assessment (1940), Pascal on the reminiscence technique (1954), Ohl on *Stopfkuchen* (1964), and Helmut Richter on the *Chronik* (1966) — will be mentioned in later chapters; Martini's essay on *Prinzessin Fisch* was touched upon above. But something can be said of the volume as an axial work joing past achievements and future directions. It opens with an essay on *Stopfkuchen* by Romano Guardini (1932). It is not quite clear why Helmers put this essay at the head of the new views, as it is not very illuminating and largely retells the story; furthermore, Fehse had found reason to praise it as a naive response undistorted by the spirit of research (Fehse 1934, 101). Erich Weniger's essay of 1951, which assesses Raabe's relationship to bourgeois life through his vocabulary, calls particular attention to the level of anxiety and misery and the sense of impending catastrophe in the external world and argues that he wore only the mask of the bourgeoisie. Herman Meyer's article of 1953 explains that plot elements in Raabe are relativized "zugunsten des übertatsächlichen Sinngehalts" (Helmers 1968a, 118), and that his manner of narration — he is speaking of the *Chronik* and *Stopfkuchen* here, but the point is extendable to Raabe's habits generally — breaks up the end-oriented intentionality of story-telling (121).

Meyer, one of the most accomplished of the several Netherlanders who turn up in our history, became known with a book on

Der Sonderling in der deutschen Dichtung, which, for understandable reasons was not much noticed when it was first published in 1943, so that the second edition of 1963 is usually employed. A large portion of this book is devoted to Raabe. Meyer is a lucid, sensitive, and humane scholar, and there are many acute observations in his chronological tour through Raabe's career. I think, however, that the topic is a little unfortunate. The "Sonderling," the "Kauz," the crotchety odd fellow had long been a cliché of discourse about Raabe. Like much of the twaddle about "humor," it tends to trivialize him somewhat, and it obscures the movement of oppositional figures in the fiction to form alternative communities with one another. Meyer concludes with a segment on the opposition of "Gesellschaft" and "Gemeinschaft" (Meyer 1963, 289), a vocabulary that introduces an ideological matrix that is not congruent with Raabe. With him it is not a matter of opposing natural, organic, integrated "Gemeinschaft" against artificial, civilized, alienated "Gesellschaft"; his "Gemeinschaften" are unnatural, counter-normative, willed and chosen by humane, tolerant people in mutual sympathy with one another and in resistance to the harshness and petty egotism of naturally evolved society.

But that was not all that Meyer had to say about Raabe. In 1961 he produced the tour-de-force of his career, a book on the poetics of quotation in the European novel; the English version of 1968 is itself a tour-de-force of translation. Mention has already been made of Fritz Jensch's long hunt for identifications of Raabe's allusions and quotations, but Meyer puts this device into its cultural-historical context, showing how writers alienated and ironized the banal bourgeois habit of citing the tag lines of the cultural patrimony upon any conceivable stimulus (Meyer 1968, 18-19). His example from Raabe is, appositely, *Hastenbeck,* but he begins with a general estimation of some five thousand quotations in Raabe's œuvre, yielding one every second page; this habit

> plays a decisive part in determining the stylistic physiognomy of his narrative art, to a degree that probably can scarcely be equaled in the works of any other German or non-German writer. (204-05)

Once again Meyer argues that "the structure of the narrative is not, or scarcely at all, determined by the pragmatic lower level, but rather by the ideal upper realm" (213).

To skip for a moment to the other Netherlander in Helmers's volume, Frank C. Maatje, he, too, is best known for a major work apart from the item included here, an analysis of space in *Der Hungerpastor* (Maatje 1961b). In 1964 Maatje published one of the basic works in any library of novel theory, *Der Doppelroman*, a study of duplicative narrative structures. His choice from Raabe is, perhaps a little oddly, the *Chronik*, which he treats as a case of incomplete duplication, nevertheless pointing to the three actions of past, present, and of writing, all taking place in the same space, and the dialectic of distance and nearness (Maatje 1964, 37-52).

From 1961 Helmers also included an essay of Hoppe, "Wilhelm Raabe einst und heute," actually a revisionary account of Raabe's career, correcting and resetting accents misplaced in the past. Johannes Klein's paper of the following year on *Die Gänse von Bützow* takes an unusual tack by detecting a dramatic structure in the novella, claiming that it has often been given staged readings that bring out a hidden comedy in the work (Klein 1962, 99-100). Raabe thought about writing dramas, the literary genre with the highest prestige at that time, but he stuck with his exclusive profession of writing fiction; the discovery of dramatic structure within one or another of his works widens his accomplishment still more. In 1980 Dieter Arendt would interpret Raabe's authorial interventions as dramatic sallies against objective narration, putting the readership in the role of a theater audience (Arendt 1980c).

Heinrich A. Stammler, a German scholar at the University of Kansas, writing on irony and pathos in *St. Thomas*, takes the opportunity to show how Raabe's symbolism transcends the fashions of historical fiction, and points out that despite the transfiguration of Camilla into a heroine and of Leflerus into an Old Testament prophet, nothing is allowed to relieve the meaninglessness and viciousness of the historical event (Helmers 1968a, 200-10). A two-part article that appeared in the *Raabe-Jahrbuch* in 1962 and 1963 by Gerhart Mayer offers an outline of an interpretation of *Altershausen*. It makes some good points about the narrative originality and the possible direction of the fragment, but as it takes the retarded, whiny Ludchen as a harmoniously cheerful, childlike figure and the pale, passive Minchen as one of Raabe's finest female figures (Mayer 1962, 1963), I have not found it of much use. More substantial is Walter Killy's 1963 analysis of the expressive structure, the lattice of symbols, and the transformation of the (fully researched) historical facts into historically organized signs in *Das Odfeld*. This model interpretation, which first appeared in *Der deutsche Roman: Vom Barock bis zur Gegenwart*, edited by Benno von Wiese, and in Killy's *Wirklichkeit und Kunstcharakter: Neun Romane des 19. Jahrhunderts*, both in 1963, was republished in the new edition of the latter, *Romane des 19. Jahrhunderts: Wirklichkeit und Kunstcharakter* in 1967.

From 1964 the volume contains an article by Hans Oppermann on the great variety of the management of time levels in Raabe's narration. Oppermann (1895-1982) was one of the last of those who memory reached back into Raabe's time. He did not know Raabe personally, but vividly recalled his funeral (E 4: 318-19). He published numerous articles and commentaries on our author, regularly keeping his eye on the principle that "Raabe ist nicht Prediger und nicht Philosoph, er ist in erster Linie Künstler, Dichter" (Oppermann 1961, 39). As a classical philologist he was able to produce the best essay on Raabe's relationship to antiquity, in which he breaks with the past habit of elevating him by ascribing humanistic *Bildung* to him, describes the range as well as the limits of his knowledge, and shows that his classical allusions were realistic rather than idealistic with his eye kept on the cultural patrimony, as always, as a record of oppression and suffering (Oppermann 1966). In 1970 Oppermann produced the *rororo bildmonographie* on Raabe. These volumes are less introductions to systematic study, like the Sammlung Metzler, than resources for the harrassed teacher who is obliged to deal with an imperfectly mastered topic; if all else fails, the pictures can be shown. For this reason I am gratefully attached to the series. Oppermann's workmanlike, straightforward volume suits the purpose exactly and will not mislead the user. Its only fault is a brief, excessively extenuating account of the reception history, separating it from its Nazi component and justifying it as legitimate in its own way (Oppermann 1970, 131-32). *Raabe in neuer Sicht* concludes with an essay of the editor Helmers from 1965 addressing the question of who narrates his stories, explaining why it cannot be the author as the cultists assumed, and attempting a typology of his narrative modes.

I have gone into such detail on Helmers's volume and some of the other work radiating from it in order to exhibit it as a symptomatic event. From now on it will not be possible to cover the critical history with anything like this thoroughness, for the revival has naturally brought with it a great expansion of scholarly and critical literature. The *Raabe-Jahrbücher* of the 1960s averaged 147 pages; of the '70s, 171; of the '80s, 228. German literary scholarship tends to burgeon in anniversary years, so that there was a great bulge in Raabe criticism to acknowledge his 150th birthday in 1981. The volume of papers published by Leo A. Lensing and Hans-Werner Peter on that occasion alone contained thirty-three articles. Therefore what follows will be but a quick overview of some publications that appeared after Raabe's reputation had been recognizably reestablished.

Karl Hoppe collected a number of his more important contributions under the title of *Wilhelm Raabe: Beiträge zum Verständnis seiner Person und seines Werkes* in 1967. It contains biographical research, for example on Raabe's two years as an auditor at the University of Berlin and the corrected circumstances of his move from Stuttgart to Braunschweig in 1870; some additional correspondence; the republication of the edited aphorisms; an account of Raabe's manuscripts and papers; along with several interpretive studies and general assessments.

In the following year a major interpretive monograph appeared: Eduard Beaucamp, *Literatur als Selbstdarstellung: Wilhelm Raabe und die Möglichkeiten eines deutschen Realismus*. For Beaucamp, Raabe's realism consists in a struggle with reality. He notes the contrast of his narrative presence and the validity of his fictional world with the objectlessness of his personal life (Beaucamp 1968, 16). The reality in his work is so far shaped by the needs of his consciousness that the definition of his "realism" is difficult unless it includes his self-realization as a narrator (73-74). Beaucamp has a good deal to say about the ambiguity of the imagination as, on the one hand, the source of art and of transcendental vision and, on the other, as a threat of self-delusion and irrationality, a point on which I have thought Raabe might be compared with Keller. His work was so personal as to make communication difficult (207). Beaucamp is especially clear on

Raabe's co-optation of the reader and his efforts to manage reader response (220-22). This mature study is not only a sign of the advances taking place at that time but continues to be of value as an introduction to Raabe's realism as a narratological problem.

More noticed at the time and more influential was another study of 1968, Hubert Ohl's *Bild und Wirklichkeit: Studien zur Romankunst Raabes und Fontanes*, perhaps because it is grounded in Hegel's theory of the novel, which is the way German literary scholars like to go about things. It might be mentioned parenthetically that the yoking of Raabe with Fontane is another sign of his upgrading; in fact, Ohl rightly sees Raabe's creative range within the genre of the novel as greater than Fontane's. Nevertheless, in retrospect Ohl's study may strike us as more conventional than others of the time. He is committed to the principle of the wholeness of the work of art, all the aspects of which reflect its structural form (Ohl 1968, 12). I rather doubt the utility of the principle in this case, in view of the disparateness of Raabe's formal experimentalism. Also, given his isolation in his time, I would see him as less exemplary for the evolution of the nineteenth-century German novel than Ohl does (18). He treats Raabe's main characters as "Sonderlinge"; I have already indicated why I think this view inadequate. One can see at such points that the discussion lurks in the shadow not only of Hegel but also of Goethe. With an evaluation that has become conventional, Ohl concentrates exclusively, with the exception of the *Chronik*, on the late works. Yet he has valuable things to say on Raabe's failure to achieve the *Bildungsroman* (in respect of which he *is* typical of his time); his struggle with the *Zeitroman*; and his difficulty in maintaining a transcendental dimension, which he eventually achieves by dissolving event into its meaning, but only within the finite limits of the story.

A sensible Bern dissertation by Eduard Klopfenstein, published in 1969, examines the relationship of narrator and reader. Here the early works are given more attention, as they exhibit the structures more clearly. Klopfenstein regards the self-aware reflection on narrative procedure as a notably original feature, but this is because he does not give sufficient attention to Raabe's English models. After summarily treating the whole career, Klopfenstein examines first and third-person narrations separately in each of four phases, attempting to show a development in search of greater precision. Raabe's modernity lies in his awareness of the aporias of the narrator-reader relationship and of the impossibility of omniscience and objectivity.

This tendency to see Raabe as a harbinger of the modern is countered somewhat by the 1970 Stuttgart dissertation of Karl Hotz, another of the several studies of space. This seems to have been a modish topic for a while, though in Raabe's case those addressing it seem to wind up talking about something else; in general Hotz employs Raabe's space and settings as threads on which to hang a sequence of interpretations. He is, however, less modernist than some other interpreters, and offers a warning that might well be taken to heart:

> Indem man Raabes ohne Zweifel vorhandene Gesellschafts-kritik herausstellt, wird man wieder nur *einem* Raabe, nämlich dem, den man *will,* gerecht, nicht aber seiner höchst differenzierten und polyphonen Erzählkunst, (Hotz 1970, 126)

and he criticizes Helmers, not unjustly, for introducing this tendency. Yet another space study, by Rolf-Dieter Koll in 1977, stays somewhat more on the point, inquiring how spaces function as aspects of story-telling and concentrating on *Die Leute aus dem Walde, Alte Nester,* and *Die Akten des Vogelsangs* as being each at the end of a development from non-symbolic, realistic spaces to their employment as objective correlatives, becoming less real and more symbolic. Koll mounts an unusual comparison to Cézanne and the style that led to cubism (Koll 1977, 90), a complex into which he also integrates Raabe's drawings (159-63). I am skeptical about this as I am about a number of Koll's interpretations, but his work remains valuable since he has an unusual sense of the literary and artistic character of Raabe's writing.

Monographs on individual works become rarer in this phase, but Karl Jürgen Ringel's Marburg dissertation of 1970 gives detailed attention to the motifs and images in Raabe's last completed work, the historical novel *Hastenbeck.* Ringel brings out Raabe's struggle in this work for optimism, tempered by "die Einsicht in die Bedingtheit und Fragwürdigkeit des Daseins" (Ringel 1970, 60). One must appreciate peace but understand it only as a matter of temporary appearance. As a historical novel *Hastenbeck* is unusual in that it is focused on a defeat (or, I would be more inclined to say, a pointless standoff); events are driven by an un-Christian transcendental fate, and are pushed into the background in favor of the existential problematic. There is much of value in this study, though I should like to have seen a little more about *Hastenbeck* as a revision and perhaps repudiation of *Der Schüdderump,* a point merely brushed (51), and on the vision of the German cultural renaissance already gestating in this gloomy mid-eighteenth-century context. Ringel reviews the faults of the older reception in an appendix; like many novice scholars he is a little hard on some of his predecessors, especially Perquin and Martini (149-55), and when he characterizes Barker Fairley's work (about which more in the next chapter) as "mehr eine einfühlsame Studie als eine wissenschaftlichen Ansprüchen genügende Arbeit" (171), I think he has been deceived by Fairley's easy-going style.

The last critical work on which I wish to comment here is Dieter Kafitz's study of the constellation of figures as a mode of apprehending reality in the work of Freytag, Spielhagen, Fontane, and Raabe, published in 1978. This study is important on account of its comparative dimension, dealing with the realism problem in the second half of the nineteenth century not so much from a theoretical base but from the practice of the writers; it also deserves credit for recalling attention to Spielhagen, a novelist whose current neglect is in no way proportional to his importance in his own time. Kafitz foregrounds the historical, more precisely, the political context. Raabe, he argues, valued the elitist individual over the community, freedom over equality; he was thus not a democrat, and his sympathy with workers was not socialist, though his novels are in their effect (as opposed to their intention) "'demokratisch,' weil sie realistisch sind" (Kafitz 1978, 229). On the whole, however, Raabe is seen as less of a proto-modernist and more of a conservative in his own time, committed to bourgeois-liberal views that are becoming increasingly obsolete and contribute to the split between his positive characters and their social environment:

Die Figurenkonstellation macht die Grundtendenzen der Zeit transparent: das Auseinanderfallen von bürgerlich liberalen Wertvorstellungen und staatlich-gesellschaftlicher Ordnung. (229)

Kafitz's book exhibits the (in this case, mostly positive) effects of the systematic politicization of literary-critical discourse that had taken place in West Germany during the preceding decade. This is a topic that I intend to look at more closely two chapters hence.

In concluding this chapter I just want to mention two other areas of advance during this perod. One is the increasing availability of scholarly *Realien*. Under this heading I would put various biographical studies and discoveries, such as those found in Karl Hoppe's volume of collected papers. Another interesting example is the effort of Else Hoppe to clarify as far as possible the relationship between Raabe and his best friend's wife, Marie Jensen (Hoppe 1966). As we shall see later on, this has become a somewhat contentious matter in Raabe studies; my own view is that Else Hoppe's cautious and moderate claims are well worth considering. A welcome removal of an old, willful misunderstanding is Dieter Arendt's article in the *Heine-Jahrbuch* of 1980 on Raabe's positive and fairly extensive relationship to Heine (Arendt 1980a). Of particular value to students was the publication of a paperback *Studienausgabe* in 1981 by Hans-Werner Peter, for which some established and some younger Raabe scholars were called upon: Peter himself for the *Chronik* and *Die Akten des Vogelsangs*, Elisabeth Walbert for *Horacker;* Joachim Müller and Peter for *Das Horn von Wanza;* William T. Webster for *Pfisters Mühle* and *Stopfkuchen;* Günter Heumann for *Unruhige Gäste;* Leo A. Lensing for *Im alten Eisen;* Peter Ensthaler for *Das Odfeld*. The thoroughly annotated volumes represent a useful middle choice between the standard scholarly edition and the individual texts that appear in various formats from time to time. Unfortunately it is now out of print. In 1985 Hans-Jürgen Schrader brought out a ten-volume paperback edition, which I have not seen. In keeping with current preferences it concentrates on late works, which is reasonable enough, but it was perhaps not such a good idea to exclude the *Chronik,* also of value for students.

Finally, another area of inquiry, a most necessary one, was the examination of the history of the Raabe-Gesellschaft. As I mentioned earlier, this began with Töteberg and Zander's article in the 1973 *Jahrbuch,* which traces the Nazified discourse back to the ideological foundations of the society. Then in 1977 Eugen Rüter published a monograph history of the society, originally an Aachen dissertation of 1975. This is a heavily theoretical work that charts

text types from the *Mitteilungen* and generally exhibits its origins
in the neo-Marxist phase of West German scholarship. Its chief
weakness, as was pointed out in a detailed review (Schrader 1977),
is an effort to arraign the Raabe scholars and the society's membership of today by association with the ideological pattern of the past,
thus flattening as far as possible the changes that have taken place
in the modern phase of criticism and in some cases ascribing to
modern scholars positions that they have in fact combatted.
Nevertheless, it is a valuable source of information about the
founding and early character of the Raabe-Gesellschaft and the kind
of discourse it sponsored. On the seventy-fifth anniversary of the
society in 1986 Horst Denkler delivered at the annual meeting a
less confrontational and more palliative retrospect, which nevertheless puts considerable stress on the efforts of the disciples to
suppress exogenous criticism and control the discourse (Denkler
1987a). This topic may not be exhausted, but, as I have indicated, it
perhaps should be taken up comparatively.

4: The Anglo-American Initiative

THIS CHAPTER ADDRESSES AN AREA of criticism that has been separated from the foregoing with a little difficulty, but that I believe deserves separate treatment because of its relative magnitude and the impulses it has given: Raabe study from Britain, Canada, and the United States. To be sure, Anglo-American criticism and scholarship have for a long time and especially since World War II been a significant presence in German literary studies, although there have been signs recently that its importance, at least as seen from within the German-speaking cultures, has been receding. In the peculiar case of Raabe, however, Anglo-American criticism has been on the front line of the process of rehabilitation, and there is a sense in which the modern main line of German criticism has become adapted to Anglo-American evaluations and methodological habits. The magnitude of this influence has been somewhat obscured to the naked eye by the circumstance that most British and some American dissertations have remained unpublished — a symptom, perhaps, at least in the American cases, of the continuing insecurity of Raabe's place in the post-war canon. But when all the material, most though not all of it in the English language is taken into account, its quantity and quality are impressive, and once again we will be reduced to adumbrations and selective sketches that cannot claim to be exhaustive.

The question arises why, given the barriers to Raabe's reception and the fact that, outside of the German field, he is virtually unknown to Anglo-American literary culture, he should have turned out to be such an attractive and stimulating object of criticism. One reason may be that Anglo-American scholars are less immediately burdened by the cultural and intellectual complicities that have made *Germanistik* and its history so problematic within German culture, and another that, at least until relatively recently, Anglo-American critics have not been as much inclined to foreground ideological and political considerations in evaluative response. But my explanation is that, although Raabe may be initially unknown to English-speaking readers, once he does become known, he is easy to recognize as a writer in our most familiar tradition. This is owing, I believe, in no small part to his aloofness from his contemporary German literary context and his demonstrable orientation on English fiction, especially of Thackeray. This does not, of course, mean that he is deracinated from his German social and historical context — that is emphatically not the case — but his formal modelling on English fiction leads to an effect that has caused me to call him "a German *Victorian* writer" (Sammons 1987, xi). If this is as accurate as I believe it to be, then it is not difficult to understand why readers for whom the Victorian novel is a classical segment of their literary patrimony develop an affinity for Raabe often marked by an unusual degree of enthusiasm and verve.

The first American scholarly studies of Raabe were two papers by Walter Silz published in 1924. One deals with the postulated relationship of *Der Hungerpastor* with Gustav Freytag's *Soll und Haben*, a persistently touchy topic, as we shall see. Silz pairs characters, leaves the matter of actual influence open, and reasonably observes that "Raabe's whole book surpasses Freytag's in poetic richness" (Silz 1924a, 10). The other is a treatment of pessimism in the Stuttgart trilogy, in which Silz appears to make the three novels even more gloomy than they are in fact. On the whole, his attitude toward Raabe is rather cool and distanced, as in this characteristic judgment: "As a creator of characters, Raabe displays a favoritism, inartistically apparent at times, for the man of retiring sensitiveness and dreamy imagination" (Silz 1924b, 691). Following Silz's papers, there appeared another on Raabe's figuration of the emigrant to America (Coenen 1937).

A more ambitious effort was Kathryn Louise Albaugh's Stanford dissertation of 1941 on Thackeray's influence. She summarizes the history of Thackeray's very considerable reputation in Germany, pointing out significantly that the pope of objective narration, Julian Schmidt, did not approve of him and almost inevitably called up the ghost of Jean Paul (Albaugh 1941, 32). She reviews the similarities and differences (especially in social level) of the biographies of the two writers, and then seeks for similar constellations of characters, plot motifs, and themes; she makes the rather remarkable claim that "three-fifths of Raabe's characters have been definitely colored by prototypes to be found in Thackeray's works" (221). Although some such filiations do exist, this is in general not a very satisfactory way of dealing with the relationship, which, as Julian Schmidt's disapproval might well indicate, was more a matter of narrative technique, tone, and perspective. In places Albaugh seems excessively dependent on Fehse, not surprisingly in a study of that date. Nevertheless, there is much in her dissertation that is thoughtfully observed; it should be the basis of any future treatment of this important, still incompletely researched topic.

After this Raabe remained pretty much dormant in English-language criticism until after World War II. There were some scattered dissertations in the 1950s and 1960s, some by German nationals studying in the United States (Lensing 1981b). However, the new era may be said to have really opened with a remarkable intervention by the prestigious Canadian Germanist Barker Fairley (1887-1986), well known for his graceful, urbane studies of Goethe and Heine. In 1952 he published a paper entitled "The Modernity of Wilhelm Raabe," republished three years later in German translation in the *Mitteilungen* (Fairley 1952, 1955). A more precisely prophetic utterance would be hard to find in the modern criticism of any topic. Fairley definitely shifted the emphasis to Raabe's multiperspectival narrative technique, which compraises all the variants of the narrator-reader relationship and "touches, at one point or another, all the forms that fiction can take"; Raabe possessed a "general awareness from the start, of what is involved mentally in the process of narration" (Fairley 1952, 74). Fairley admitted that Raabe's excellence in this regard was not the prevailing view of literary scholarship, but asserted with eminent prescience: "the prevailing view will have to go" (74). Logically, he also foresaw the shift of interest from the early to the late works (81). In 1961 Fairley published a full-length monograph, alertly translated into German in the same year. Here he takes up the modern theme of Raabe's wavering between the search for his own voice and for success by trying to write like the others. Fairley's individual readings, though always worth our consideration, are less important today than the respect for Raabe's literary artistry implied by his interpretive attention. Over the years he made a number of other contributions to the cause, among them an

English students' edition of *Pfisters Mühle* in 1956 and a "Nach-wort" to a German paperback edition of the *Chronik* in 1966. Fair-ley's English counterpart in breaking new ground was Roy Pascal, whose paper on the "reminiscence technique" appeared in 1954; its importance was recognized by its inclusion in German translation in Helmers's *Raabe in neuer Sicht*. Pascal sees the reminiscence technique as an evaluative canon and is therefore naturally drawn to the late works, especially *Stopfkuchen*; unlike most critics who have followed this line, he is rather cool to the *Chronik*. He was one of the first — perhaps *the* first — to be reminded by *Die Akten des Vogelsangs* of Thomas Mann's *Doktor Faustus* (Pascal 1954, 345). This is another initiative that deserves to be followed up further; although Raabe was not a conscious model for Mann as Fontane was, in terms of literary history he is certain discussible as a predecessor. However, Pascal was a man of the Left, and as such his enthusiasm for Raabe was considerably tempered by social and ideological considerations: it is Raabe's weakness that his social range was narrow (339, 348), and the "impact of the masses ... scarcely appears, even where it seems to demand attention" (348). This reticence also appears in the chapter on Raabe in Pascal's book of 1956, *The German Novel*, one of the main resources for that topic in English. Here Raabe receives distinctly muted praise: his "work, subdued in tone and modest in intellectual scope, has a solidity and integrity that, as time goes by, raise it more and more above that of his contemporaries" (Pascal 1956, 143). He "never shows much narrative skill" (163), a judgment remarkably at odds with a fundamental insight of modern, especially Anglo-Saxon criticism. Pascal is not much interested in the aesthetics of nar-ration, a sign, perhaps, of his discipleship to Lukács (177), about whom there will be more to say in the next chapter. Pascal devotes a whole section to Raabe's limitations (173-77), in itself a reasonable consideration, although most Anglo-American critics have come to a more enthusiastic level of appreciation. Nevertheless, he has contributed one of the major studies of *Altershausen* (Pascal 1962), in which he addresses the most fundamental question about that text: why it remained a fragment. He finds much of the solution in the misconception of the character of Ludchen Bock. This view has been controversial and has, I think, not become the majority position, but I believe it is correct.

Another at least partly English-language critic who has caught the attention of German scholarship is Marketa Goetz-Stankiewicz (her name varies) of the University of British Columbia. She first emerged in 1962 with an article on the relatively neglected topic of Raabe's short stories (though some are what others would call novellas), in which she makes the now familiar claims for his modernity, putting him, in fact, in quite elevated company:

> ... his old-fashioned ways are deceptive. He is a modern writer. Like Kafka, he is acutely conscious of the dark places of the human mind; like Camus, he tries to fathom the absurdity of man's position; like Thomas Mann, he muses about the effects of spiritual isolation; like Virginia Woolf, he tackles the same problems over and over again, striving to reach the lighthouse of spiritual harmony. (Goetz 1962, 67)

More noticed was an ingenious and original effort of 1968 to divide Raabe's character types into the unresolved antithesis of the "tailor," who covers men up and beautifies, and the "sweeper," who delves below the surface, sometimes finding emptiness (Stankiewicz 1968). This essay was republished in German translation in the *Raabe-Jahrbuch* (Goetz-Stankiewicz 1972) and is intermittently cited with admiration.

In the 1960s there began to appear a series of mostly unpublished dissertations. One of these was Geoffrey Patrick Guyton Butler's study of "England and America in the Writings of Wilhelm Raabe." This quite long and thorough opus can serve as a reference resource for Raabe's interests in this area. It deals with his views and representations of these nations and their people, his grasp of the English language, his wide knowledge of English literature and the echoes and influences from it, and his quite extensive personal connections to English and American individuals. There is much useful material here. It is extraordinary how many English and American literary figures can be adduced in such an inquiry: not only the expected ones, Shakespeare and Sterne, Dickens and Thackeray, but also Bunyan, Lamb, Milton, Macpherson ("Ossian"), Defoe, Fielding, Scott, Irving, Marryat, Cooper, Poe, Harriet Beecher Stowe, etc. Butler, however, has not given the last word on these matters. He seems to lack a sense of humor about Raabe's practices of quotation and allusion; he shows that many of the allusions come from quotation anthologies, but he is not alert to their parodistic function as the tag lines of philistine culture. He considers Dickens more important and more congenial than Thackeray, arguing that Albaugh's claims in regard to Thackeray are exaggerated (Butler 1961, 225, 275, 338-40), but in this I think he is mistaken because he has not asked the most pertinent narratological questions. The study is an impressive achievement all the same.

In 1967 William P. Hanson, a senior lecturer at the University of Exeter, began a series of thoughtful, carefully wrought papers, with some observations, clearly directed against the view of Raabe as a static, conservative, backward-looking writer, by arguing that he was "fascinated by the idea of change and movement" and, "with monumental integrity," sincerely tolerant and open-ended in his beliefs (Hanson 1967/68, 124, 125) In the meantime Hanson has published in the *Raabe-Jahrbuch* on the *Chronik* and *Der Marsch nach Hause* (Hanson 1983, 1985a), on Raabe's poems and the geography of his settings (Hanson 1985b, 1986). Of particular interest is an unusual comparison, written for the Lensing/Peter anniversary volume in 1981, of Raabe with Thomas Hardy, taking as his examples the nearly contemporary *Unruhige Gäste* and *The Woodlanders*. Comparisons of this kind continue to be, I believe, the most useful in defining Raabe's literary-historical location as a novelist.

A 1968 dissertation from the University of California at Berkeley by Monica Weber Clyde takes up again the question of the idea of *Bildung;* she is, naturally, dissatisfied with her predecessor Helmers for lack of depth (Clyde 1968, 8). Like many other observers, Clyde sees Raabe struggling for his own voice while having to make concessions to his public. She finds him sensitive to the stunting of the personality behind a façade of *Bildung* (36). Although she sees *Der Hungerpastor* as an effort to write a *Bildungsroman*, she argues that he possessed no humanistic concept of *Bildung* but was wholly focused on practical wisdom (65). Clyde continues with perceptive, rather critical analyses of *Alte Nester* and *Stopfkuchen*, and mounts a thoughtful comparison with Freytag in regard to the ideology of *Bildung* (128-30). Ultimately she sees Raabe participating in a new, intense

Kult des Individuums. In der starken Betonung der Individualität liegt seine romantische Grundstimmung, die

jedoch durch den Realismus seiner illusionslosen Lebens-
haltung aufgewogen wird. (139)

Another in the sequence of British dissertations was Stanley
Radcliffe's "The Figure of the Eccentric in the Work of Wilhelm
Raabe and its Significance for his Literary Achievement," completed at the University of Bristol in 1970 but not published until
1984 and then in German translation. In the intervening years
Radcliffe established himself as a presence in Raabe scholarship,
contributing essays on the theme of the Thirty Years War in *Else
von der Tanne* (Radcliffe 1969), on Raabe's interest in the railroad
(Radcliffe 1974), on one of his Braunschweig clubs (Radcliffe 1978),
on the historical background of *Im Siegeskranze* (Radcliffe 1979,
republished in German 1981), on his handwritten copy of an
English translation of a poem by Jensen (Radclife 1982b), and on the
diary (Radcliffe 1982a). This work has been solid and learned, but
not very imaginative. In fact, it has tended to reinforce traditional
views of Raabe as a local, backward-looking, quietistic writer
withdrawn from society. This posture is evident in the very theme
of the dissertation, the *Sonderling*, with which Radcliffe, who
identifies more than sixty examples in the works (Radcliffe 1984,
32), intends to be a successor to Herman Meyer but which, as I have
remarked, leads to a foreshortened view of the social implications
of Raabe's characterization.

Radcliffe tends to unliterary surface readings of characters as
incarnations of attitudes toward life without much sense of texture
or the crosscurrents of irony, and the German version is marred by
a number of misspelled character's names and other errors, though
that may not be the author's fault. The imposition upon Raabe of
the classically conservative distinction of *Gesellschaft* and *Gemeinschaft* (128) is a further example of putting him in a regressive
light. Another is the essay on the railroad, which gives an unfortunately misleading impression of him as a traditionalist resisting
modern developments. The truth is that he was fascinated by tech-
nological developments in transportation and communication,
and he was an admirer of the railroad. Here as elsewhere Radcliffe
seems unable to distinguish among the voices of author, narrator,
and characters. Perhaps his evaluation of Raabe as a minor writer
(Radcliffe 1974, 131) has limited his own perceptions.

If Radcliffe's feelings about Raabe are tepid, those of H. R. Klieneberger are downright contemptuous; he is the most dismissive English-language writer on Raabe in the modern phase of criticism. His 1969 essay on Dickens and Raabe is part of a larger comparative study of the English and German novel that appeared in 1981. I suspect the whole project of being ideologically driven, to belittle the German novel tradition. Certainly the essay on Raabe is little more than a polemic, devaluing him in favor of Dickens at every turn in regard to such matters as sensuality, female characterization, political awareness, receptivity to technology, cosmopolitanism, transcendence of class, plausibility, strength, breadth, etc. The tendentiousness shows itself especially in the juxtaposition of an indictment of Raabe's treatment of Jewish figures with an exculpation of Dickens's "embodiment of general villainy" (Klieneberger 1969, 97-98). More judicious considerations of this matter are possible (see, for example, Gelber 1979). Certainly it is permissible to prefer Dickens to Raabe, but a genuinely comparative consideration might detect some merits in the latter, for example, in his resistance to Dickens's moralistically melodramatic characterization. Klieneberger complains that Raabe ascribes eccentricity and isolation to his protagonists, while Dickens never does, making only his villains eccentric (Klieneberger 1969, 112-13). I have wondered elsewhere why this difference should be held against Raabe "unless it is believed that readers should not be troubled in their moral certainties" (Sammons 1987, 165). Indeed, it seems to me that Raabe is in many ways less affirmative than Dickens of the superintending values of his society.

The sequence of British dissertations resumes with Gerald Opie's 1971 study of childhood in Raabe's works from the University of Exeter. For Opie, the original paradise of childhood and its "loss as the fall from grace, lies at the root of all of Raabe's writing" (Opie 1971, 4). Opie observes that Raabe's "attitude to the child becomes increasingly complex" (126), but he perceives on the whole an allegiance to the child realm as against that of the adult. Childhood is associated with naivety, wholeness, acceptance, and passivity; the matured Just Everstein in *Alte Nester* is said to be paradoxically childlike (144), while the alleged childish naivety of Phöbe in *Unruhige Gäste*, in what I believe to be a serious misinterpretation, is said to do positive harm (179). Opie makes stimulating if sometimes debatable observations on *Die Akten des Vogelsangs* and *Stopfkuchen,* and he sees the problem in *Alterhausen* with special clarity: "Perhaps in no other work has Raabe given such a striking illustration of the undesirability of the childhood idyll's continuation into adult life" (222). Opie is an alert reader — he contributed to the Lensing/Peter volume an observant essay on the simultaneous presence of tolerance and satire in *Der Dräumling* (Opie 1981). But in his dissertation he seems sometimes rather airily dismissive of Raabe's narrative strategies — for example, in regard to disfunctional family life (Opie, 1971, 31) or the aporias of heredity, environment, and individual responsibility (81) — rather than asking how they function and what sort of realistic insights they reflect.

Around this time a series of American dissertations began to appear. In 1973 Michael Lee Ritterson completed at Harvard an orderly, precise study of narrators and narration in six third-person novels: *Horacker, Das Horn von Wanza, Unruhige Gäste, Im alten Eisen, Das Odfeld,* and *Hastenbeck.* The elegantly written study, despite its rather austere formalism, is driven by rational observation that behind the texts there might actually be an author:

> the similarities established in a systematic investigation would in all likelihood admit the definition of an authorial identity coexistent with the several narrator-identities. One would then be compelled to speak of Wilhelm Raabe as the creative agent common to all the works. This identification of the authorial presence would, in my view, in no way compromise the importance of the narrators and their function in the several novels. (Ritterson 1973, 381)

Ritterson published a version of his work on *Das Odfeld* and *Hastenbeck* in the 1976 *Raabe-Jahrbuch,* but not the whole study.

In 1974 Katherine Starr Kaiser at Brown University completed an examination of the six *Krähenfelder Geschichten: Zum wilden Mann, Höxter und Corvey, Eulenpfingsten, Frau Salome, Die Innerste,* and *Zum alten Proteus,* which collectively represent a high point of Raabe's art of the novella. Kaiser pursues a careful, thoughtful analysis consonant with the subtleties of these stories. She ascribes the complexity of Raabe's narrative perspective to his commitment to truthfulness (Kaiser 1974, 7). She shows how the third-person narrator is constructed like a first-person narrator in

regard to the undermining of narrative conventions, the interpola-
tion of wise observations, the visible manipulation of symbolism,
the attribution of significance to the historical, and the
management of time levels. In my opinion this is the best study of
the *Krähenfelder Geschichten* as a group yet accomplished, so that
it is particularly unfortunate that it has remained unpublished.
Despite its formalism it does not lose sight of meaning, of the
cautiously qualified hope Raabe meant to convey.

In 1975 another narrative study, this time of six novels of the
Stuttgart period, was completed by James Robert Reece at the
University of Oregon. Following the theoretical models especially
of Wayne Booth and Eberhard Lämmert and the interpretive
orientation of Barker Fairley and Fritz Martini, Reece also sees that
in Raabe "form has become content" (Reece 1975, 2). He stresses the
"experiment and ferment" in the Stuttgart period (27), the
"increasing 'subjectification' of the narrative" (33), increasing
frequency of authorial intrusion (38-39), and "a growing tendency ...
toward the structural manipulation of the reader's viewpoint"
(213). Reece develops an insight originally explored by Janet K.
King concerning how close the third-person narration in *Else von
der Tanne* remains to a first-person consciousness (106; cf. King
1967). Though Reece has a high regard for Raabe's narrative
artistry, he is not without criticism, for he observes that the
narrative mannerisms can sometimes be carried to excess (Reece
1975, 282). His ultimate conclusion, however, reinforces Fairley's
pioneering judgment:

> It seems Raabe is constantly aware of an entire spectrum of
> different narrative structural possibilities and chooses at
> random first one approach, then another. In doing so, he
> explores his potentials as a writer, discovers his weaknesses,
> recognizes his strong sides; as a result he establishes the firm
> foundation in his later highly complex narrative structures.
> (321)

The following year brought another narrative study, by Stephen
A. Gould at the University of Nebraska, on the rhetorical role of
the narrator in the early novels (by which he means those up to the
end of the Stuttgart period). Also inspired by Wayne Booth, he
shows how Raabe from the beginning attempts to control the

participation of the reader and create his or her role. A split in the narrative consciousness reflects a perception of discordance in reality. Gould goes far in dismantling the traditional view of Raabe as a dispenser of affirmative wisdom by paying the attention so long refused to the antinomies within the narrative voice:

> It is not at all clear that Raabe shared his narrators' beliefs. On the contrary, his use of symbol suggests that Raabe had little faith in the correspondence of real and idea, of specific empirical incident and general law of being. (Gould 1976, 34)

Gould is genuinely critical of the *Chronik;* he is the first, as far as I can see, to recognize in *Die Kinder von Finkenrode* a genuine case of an unreliable narrator; he sees the weakness of *Die Leute aus dem Walde* as a discordance between the implications of the story and the meaning the narrator tries to impose on it; and he continues with a wealth of interpretive insights, culminating in a defense of the artistic integrity of *Der Schüdderump.* While I have a high regard for all of the studies in this phase, it seems to me that Gould's is of uncommon excellence and should be one of the indispensable resources for further scholarship.

Another study of the sometimes neglected early novels is Laurel Ellen Eason's Vanderbilt University dissertation of 1979 on structure and theme. Like other observers, she finds that Raabe lost his initial narrative stance after the *Chronik;* nevertheless, she discovers clashing ambivalence in *Die Kinder von Finkenrode* and has an interesting argument concerning *Der heilige Born* that the Bohemian poet figure takes over the text as surrogate narrator (Eason 1979, 87, 110-11, 156). She does the best one can, I expect, with the dreadful *Nach dem großen Kriege* and finds *Die Leute aus dem Walde* important evidence for Raabe's struggle to find his own way (201, 203). She states wisely that, while Raabe speaks to the modern reader in form, he is a "nineteenth-century novelist at work, with a confidence in his structures and themes and a knowledge that he would reach a goal, i.e., to complete a universe of meaning" (252).

In contrast to the inclusive character of the studies just discussed, two American monographs concentrate on individual works. One is Leo A. Lensing's thorough study of *Im alten Eisen,* published in 1977. Lensing is interested in Raabe's struggle for finding and forming the right reader, his narrator's visible manipulations in contrast to the then current theory of objective narration, his pursuit of realism by stressing fictionality. He has perceptive things to say about Raabe's counter-cultural use of fairy-tale motifs, especially in regard to the truly extraordinary figuration of the street walker Rotkäppchen; about the subtle parody of the family magazine novel; and about the figure of Brokenkorb as a satire on Emanuel Geibel. This is certainly one of the best single-work studies of Raabe in any language. Although Lensing has since turned to other matters, he has made a number of further contributions to Raabe scholarship apart from his co-editorship of the 1981 anniversary volume. Some have been marked by notable originality in their objects of inquiry: a continuation of his very promising exploration of the use of fairy tales, this time focused on the *Chronik* (Lensing 1981a); an unexpected exposition of Tucholsky's interest in Raabe (Lensing 1983); and an approach to one of the enduring puzzles in Raabe's attitude, the apparent incongruity of his hostility to Naturalism with his admiration for the arch-Naturalist Zola (Lensing 1988).

The *Chronik der Sperlingsgasse* itself, generally the only work that has been exempted from the modern devaluation of Raabe's early writing, was the topic of Charlotte L. Goedsche's Northwestern University dissertation of 1980, the revised version of which was not published until 1989. Goedsche analyzes, with illuminating results, the time layers of the narration, the space structure, the forms of discourse, the involuntary recovery of memory (leading to a comparison with Proust), the self-conscious narrator, interpolated narrators, readers in the text, and the implied reader, all mobilized to support claims that the *Chronik* anticipates modernist structures and strategies. The approach is unabashedly New Critical; many of the models tend to be those who commanded critical theory in the 1950s and early 1960s. The study demonstrates the enduring power of these analytic techniques when intelligently and observantly employed, although in today's context one cannot help a feeling of anachronism.

In another way this seems to me also somewhat the case in Marilyn Sibley Fries's chapter on Raabe in her 1980 study of the image of Berlin in the German novel, originally a Yale University dissertation directed by Peter Demetz. She, too, concentrates on the *Chronik*, along with *Die Leute aus dem Walde*. She makes some very good observations on these texts, showing how in the *Chronik* the city is seen segmentally and provincially — the larger urban context is barely present — and the narrator Wachholder is rooted in a country idyll. In *Die Leute aus dem Walde* the country is also a place of security, while the city is not fully incorporated into the novel. Nevertheless, this approach tends to reinforce conventional notions about Raabe. Fries primarily delineates what the novels are *not*, thus implicitly measuring them against some model of what German realism *ought* to have been but failed to achieve. She does not sufficiently stress that in both novels the provincial prehistories are stories of misery and injustice. Furthermore, though Raabe is certainly not primarily a writer of the big city, he did not avoid or evade that setting as much as Fries's concentration on the two early works might imply. Thirteen of his works take place wholly or partly in Berlin, and several of the later works have modern, fairly gritty urban settings, notably *Im alten Eisen* and *Der Lar*.

Around this time, in 1981, Horst S. Daemmrich's Twayne volume appeared, perhaps the best first resource of information for an English-speaking reader, for whom it is *mutatis mutandis* a counterpart to Oppermann's *rororo-monographie* and Helmers's *Sammlung Metzler* volume. Daemmrich rightly stresses that Raabe was "ahead of his time in the skillful use of narrator intrusions, the use of a multiple point of view, and the far-reaching consideration of a person's response to a society in transition" (Daemmrich 1981, [7]). He is especially good on the historical fiction, pointing out that

> Raabe never states that history is unknowable, never argues against the significance of historical insight for civilized society, never counters history with a one-sided, timeless pattern of man's suffering. But he questions the false security afforded by views of historical progress, evolutionary development, and the impact of great statesmen. (76-77)

On the whole, Daemmrich's posture toward Raabe is serious and sober; rather than foregrounding his comical and satiric aspect, Daemmrich takes a somewhat conventional view of his humor as affording "the reader the exquisite pleasure of smiling at life's incongruities and laughing at human folly instead of feeling challenged to rise in defense of needed reforms" (123).

In the same year of 1981 there appeared Irene Stocksieker Di Maio's study of the third-person narratives of the Braunschweig period, originally a Louisiana State University dissertation. Di Maio argues as others have that third-person narratives can show as much multiplicity of perspective as first-person narratives (Di Maio 1981a, 32). She associates Raabe's technique with his recognition of the inevitability of change, his suspicion of absolutes, and the beginnings of a solution of "modern man's sense of inadequacy and entrapment in an increasingly complex world" in irony and humor (61, 138, 139). In a contribution to the Lensing/Peter volume, Di Maio reopened the question of Raabe's female characters, pointing out the contrast of his opinions in his personal life and the fictional figurations, and criticizing the work of Robert Anthony Graves, to which we shall come presently. The potential liveliness of this topic is demonstrated by a vigorous discussion of her paper at a symposium, recorded in the 1982 *Raabe-Jahrbuch*, 93-96.

English-speaking Germanists sometimes feel that their work will have more impact if written in German. This may be the reason why Philip James Brewster chose to do so with his 1983 Cornell University dissertation on the historical fiction. This is yet another of the certifications of Raabe's modern instincts. Brewster attests to his awareness of the questionableness of historical knowledge and objectivity and of the complexity of reality. Raabe's interests as a historical writer were not antiquarian, as were those of some of his contemporaries, and he was ironic at an early date about telling the "true story." He was skeptical about reason in history, the meaning of which, if it has one, is impenetrable to its victims. The Thirty Years War and the Seven Years War, national catastrophes to which he constantly recurred, were for him "sinn*los*" (Brewster 1983b, 217). Brewster sees clearly that Raabe hated war and generally avoided heroizing; every war was as bad as every other, and just because there had always been war did not mean that there always must be (346, 351, 366). One of the few modern scholars to give some attention to *Der heilige Born*, which has suffered from the devaluation into which all the early work has fallen, Brewster is also especially good on *Das Horn von Wanza* and *Das Odfeld*. In general, this is the best modern study on the historical fiction that constitutes about a third of Raabe's total œuvre.

To pick up again the thread of British scholarship, we may say a word about Robert Anthony Graves's University of Bristol dissertation on 1978 on female characters in Theodor Fontane and Raabe. Graves contrasts Raabe to Fontane as an inward-looking provincial (Graves 1978, 1-3). This kind of generalization is an example of Graves's tendency to operate with conventional categories, as is his employment of the concept of the *Sonderling* (43), or the kind of judgment on "woman's broad role" that Di Maio has found too undifferentiated: "to provide a source of calm and stability for those who are engaged in, or who are victims of the struggle with existence" (51). Thus he interprets the tone of the figuration of women as bourgeois, philistine, orthodox, exhibiting a "a fundamental meagreness of stance," and representing them as "basically maternal" (64-65, 276, 291, 293). These judgments rather inhibit Graves's vision. For example, he sees the "selfless devotion" of Tine's role as a wife in *Stopfkuchen* (110) but not her resistance to being overrun and silenced by her monologuing husband, nor does he sense the ambiguities in the portrayal of Klaudine in *Abu Telfan*, Frau Andres in *Die Akten des Vogelsangs*, or Phöbe in *Unruhige Gäste*. In any case, Graves's is the most gracelessly written of all the English-language studies: stiff, self-conscious, and irritatingly addicted to the passive voice.

More productive has been the work of the Scot William T. Webster, who completed his dissertation on reality and illusion in Raabe's novels at the University of Edinburgh in 1976; he then published it in German translation in 1982. In the meantime he began to emerge as one of the leading Raabe scholars of our time. Papers drawn from the dissertation appeared: one in 1978 on *Stopfkuchen* (Webster 1978); two in 1979, one on *Alte Nester* and *Altershausen*, which is particularly good on the interpretation of Ludchen Bock in the latter novel as an insecure and miserable figure, representing the illusoriness of a return to childhood (Webster 1979a, 80); the other on social change and personal insecurity (Webster 1979b). An important article in 1980 pursued the still insufficiently examined comparison with Thomas Mann, defining differences as well as similarities (Webster 1980). In the Lensing/Peter volume of 1981 he published an article on Raabe's psychopathic figures, more observant and differentiated than Maria Vogel's earlier study (Webster 1981). In the following year there appeared an essay on the motif of travel in Raabe (1982a). Webster also edited two volumes in the Lensing/Peter edition, *Stopfkuchen* and *Pfisters Mühle,* and he has been announced as co-editor of a much needed new edition of Raabe's correspondence.

The monograph based on the dissertation deals with the propensity of Raabe's characters to flight: into conformity; into the imagination, another important, insufficiently examined topic; into memory; and into extremes of character. These movements image a "Grundspannung" in the whole œuvre, an oscillation "zwischen Vision und Wirklichkeit, zwischen dem Ideellen und dem Praktischen, dem Erwünschten und dem Möglichen" (Webster 1982b, 71). Webster commands the by now indispensable sensitivity to the limited or unreliable perspectives of Raabe's narrators. He interprets *Stopfkuchen* as an attempt at a synthesis, but one that contains its own skepticism (259). On the much bandied issue of Raabe's "modernity" Webster takes the position that he should not be seen as a spirit of the twentieth century, that his world, though perhaps resisting comprehension, is not absurd (263-64).

For the sake of completeness something should doubtless be said here about my own studies, which owe no small debt to the Anglo-American critical tradition. In retrospect it appears to me that the one constant perception that informs all my work on Raabe is of the extraordinary degree of differentiation and variation in his œuvre: generic, narratological, stylistic, tonal, psychological, socio-political, and ideological. No other post-Romantic nineteenth-century German writer can match him in this variety. While it is doubtless a consequence of his energetic struggle somehow to reconcile popular success as a writer with fidelity to his own artistic instincts, the effect for us is one of constant literary experimentation. This has been most clearly seen as awareness of his narrative variety has become thematic in modern studies. But I have tried to recall in addition something often forgotten in the narratological enthusiasm, that he was *also* capable of straightforward story-telling with a subdued authorial voice, and that this variant is not necessarily inferior. I wanted to show that, while his motifs and structural strategies tend to recur, they are often very differently and sometimes antithetically employed; that his notorious "humor" should be demarcated from his less recognized comedy and satire; that he is sometimes psychologically empathic and sometimes manipulative; and — one of the odder features of the Raabe phenomenon — that the political and ideological implications of his fiction seem considerably more tolerant and generous than the apparent opinions of the private man. Like other modern critics, I have become convinced that he is a major nineteenth-century writer of European dimensions.

It is all the more incongruent that he is so little known outside German culture and the field of German literary study. Translations into English have been few; of modern ones there are only the facing-page edition of *Else von der Tanne* edited as a textbook with commentary by James C. O'Flaherty and Janet K. King in 1972, and, in The German Library, two novels in volume 45, edited by Volkmar Sander: *Horacker*, translated by John E. Woods, and *Stopfkuchen*, unfortunately titled *Tubby Schaumann*, in an old but never published translation by Barker Fairley (1983), and two novellas in volume 38, edited by myself: *Keltische Knochen* and *St. Thomas*, translated by John E. Woods (1989). In nineteenth-century England the reviews of the feeble attempts at translation were indifferent to devastating (Brill 1954/55). Sander gave to an article on the non-reception of Raabe in American and England the title "Corviana non leguntur" (Sander 1981). In a review of American scholarship Leo Lensing pointed out that it has failed to rescue Raabe "from the isolation of academic exercises and the confines of literary history" (Lensing 1981b, 534). Whether the vigor of scholarly criticism and its effect upon teaching can change this situation is difficult to say at present. It may be that Raabe, having failed to reach his international public in the nineteenth century, missed his chance.

5: The New and the Original

THE QUANTITATIVE EXPANSION OF RAABE CRITICISM in recent years, his emergence as an attractive and timely topic for scholars, both experienced and neophyte, have naturally led to intersections with the motley methodological pluralism characteristic of literary study today. This is not to say that criticism has been absorbed by modernist or post-modernist perspectives, nor do I think that this is likely to happen. Several methodological and interpretive approaches, some well established, continue to be applied side by side, including the positivistic work on the foundations, which is still being pursued. However, there are several areas in which work on Raabe has become involved with the larger currents of contemporary criticism. To discuss these matters is, of course, to attempt to fix our gaze on a flowing stream, so that much of what follows will be even more provisional than is normally necessary in an endeavor of this kind.

a: The Left

For a long time Raabe was of little interest to the Left. This is not surprising, given his intensely petty-bourgeois orientation, his Bismarckian nationalism, and his hostility to Social Democracy, more pronounced to be sure, in his private utterances than in his fiction. He seems to have had some working-class readership, and a worker defended him against a Socialist attack upon him after his death (see Sammons 1987, 105). Statistics from workers' libraries during the last years of his life show a relatively high frequency of borrowings of his books (Mikoletzky 1988, 97-99). But the estrangement must surely have grown as the Raabe cult magnified the class chauvinism and made more explicit the hostility not only to Social Democracy but to the working class itself. Upon his death Franz Mehring published a rather cool obituary, finding Raabe narrower and less worldly than Jean Paul, but less philistine than Otto Ludwig. Mehring's praise of the characterization of Moses

Freudenstein in *Der Hungerpastor* looks like a symptom of Social Democracy's insensitivity to anti-Semitism in that period (Mehring 1910, 97-99). For a generation after this, during the era of the cult, the Left had nothing more to say.

A new beginning was made by Georg Lukács, who, with his focus on nineteenth-century realism, could hardly avoid Raabe. His essay appeared in *Deutsche Realisten des 19. Jahrhunderts* in 1952 and was taken into Helmers's *Raabe in neuer Sicht*, but it was originally written in 1939 and first published in 1940, that is, deep within Lukács's most Stalinist period. As one might expect, he sees Raabe's consciousness blinded by his class location to the true determinants of history and society and to the potential of the proletariat. He associates an attempted acceptance of capitalism with aesthetic failure in *Villa Schönow* and *Pfisters Mühle* (Lukács 1952, 245-46), sees the late novels becoming ever more individualistic and apolitical (246), and characteristically worries about the German realist's provinciality, identifying "ein Schuß Philistertum, das sich an dem Erzähler Raabe künstlerisch schwer gerächt hat" and "eine bestimmte Enge and Muffigkeit" (253). His popularity, Lukács argues, was owing to his passionate but sentimental and subjective rejection of capitalism (247). Nevertheless, in some ways Lukács was surprisingly tolerant of Raabe. He recognized that in *Die Gänse von Bützow* (of which an annotated East German edition was published by Fritz Böttger in 1975) Raabe was parodying not the French Revolution but the German reaction to it (233) and found in his orientation on the spirit of the Wars of Liberation "einen plebejisch-kritischen Akzent" (234), adding that what continues to be alive in Raabe has "ständig eine plebejisch-oppositionelle Nuance" (258). He located Raabe's pessimism in a split between his national-liberal ideals and the social facts he was obliged to recognize, leading to a defensive struggle to find a corner in which inner humanity can unfold (239); thus he treats Raabe as a utopian writer. His humor is an admission of the insolubility of the problem he set himself (256). Lukács makes some perceptive observations on *Altershausen* (249), points out acutely that the protagonists of the late novels are aware of their own quixotic nature, thus bringing up the Ibsenian theme of the life-lie (250), and concedes that, though Raabe may have a modest place in literary history and will never reach the rank of Keller and

Hoffmann, he remains a significant populist writer whose roots will bring forth "Blumen und Früchte" (260-61).

Lukács, to be sure, came to be a dubious if not to say repudiated model for the cultural politics of the German Democratic Republic, where the visible interest in Raabe remained dormant until the end of the 1950s, when Helmut Richter began to write about him and edit texts in the Leipzig Reclam series. In 1963 Richter published a document of exceptional biographical interest: the Raabe file of the Schiller Foundation, from which he, and after his death, members of his family, obtained grants (Richter 1963). Beginning in 1964, together with Peter Goldammer, Richter published a six-volume edition of Raabe's works, thus certifying him as belonging to the literary patrimony of the GDR; Helmers took Richter's essay on *Die Chronik der Sperlingsgasse* from this edition into *Raabe in neuer Sicht*. To the Berlin Raabe conference of 1987 Richter contributed a learned, thoughtful essay on Raabe's relationship to the Young German movement (Richter 1988). On the *Chronik*, Walter Dietze, a prominent figure in East German literary scholarship, carried a lecture on a tour to the United States, which he published in a U. S. journal. Some of the essay betrays its provenance: Raabe's figuration of the proletariat is criticized as abstract, and there is an attack on Lukács (Dietze 1969, 339, 341). However, Dietze acknowledges the novel's pluralistic narrative perspective and praises Barker Fairley (338, 340), and in general reclaims the *Chronik* as a major nineteenth-century novel, critical of its times and open to a democratic future. An example of what could still be accomplished within the East German empirical tradition is Anneliese Klingenberg's 1984 edition of *Der Dräumling* along with all the extant documents of the Schiller centennial in Wolfenbüttel on which the novel is based, and a number of other pertinent materials from the 1859 celebrations elsewhere (Klingenberg 1984). The result is one of the most useful individual text editions of recent years.

The only full-length East German monograph on Raabe, by Hans Kolbe, appeared in 1981; some of its contents also reappeared in an article in the Lensing/Peter volume of the same year. Kolbe focuses on the Stuttgart novels and the work after 1871, thus setting himself in opposition to Lukács. He, too, acknowledges that Raabe could not see a solution in the working class and thus sought spaces of integrity within a hostile society, while at the same time remaining relentlessly opposed to "die feudale Klassenherrschaft" (Kolbe 1981a, 49); he points out rightly, however, that the notorious "Sonderling" does not drop out of society, but is *forced* out and wants nothing more than to be a normal human being (15, 173). Usefully, Kolbe locates Raabe more explicitly than other writers in the political history of nineteenth-century Germany, finding him progressively forced to abandon the hopes for harmonization still evident in *Der Hungerpastor,* turning to depictions of the failures of the bourgeoisie while falsely making timeless issues out of them. Kolbe argues that it was not Raabe's formal experimentation that estranged him from his public, but his anti-bourgeois, anti-capitalist, and anti-Prussian thrust (104). Kolbe finds the *Krähen-felder Geschichten* weak because their focus was too limited to capture "die Alltäglichkeit des Kapitalisierungsprozesses"; thus he was obliged to return to the larger form of the novel (103). Kolbe observes rightly that, in the historical fictions, war and heroism are always evaluated according to the interests of the people (124). The persuasiveness of his interpretations of individual texts varies considerably; he himself felt disadvantaged by an immature critical situation (204). The obbligato of intermittently valuable local observations over a ground bass of excessive preoccupation with the evolution of capitalism and ideological right-thinking is probably the best that could be done under the conditions prevailing in the GDR at that time. Now that this misery is thankfully at an end, it is time to write the history of East German literary criticism; when this has been done, it will be possible to see Raabe's place in it more clearly.

In the West the response of the academic Left has been a good deal more ambiguous and uncertain. In 1981 the left-wing pedagogical journal *Diskussion Deutsch* rather surprisingly devoted a large part of an issue to Raabe and, even more surprisingly, took a notably benign view of him. One touching little piece described how a schoolteacher, who had been taught to read literary theory rather than literature, stumbled across Raabe and found to his astonishment that reading could be pleasurable (Meyer, E. 1981). Another essay introduced what has become a commonplace in the modernization of Raabe: the praise of *Pfisters Mühle* as a text of prophetic ecological concern (Sporn 1981). I have expressed some skepticism about this reading (Sammons 1985a;

1988, 36-37), but it has been a step in Raabe's rehabilitation. However, the view of the Western Left has not in every case been as benign as these probes or what one must in fairness call the East German tolerance. Perhaps the most negative view in contemporary criticism is found in a 1971 study of weather imagery in bourgeois realism, originally a Berlin Technical University dissertation, by F. C. Delius, a familiar figure on the radical scene. Takings as his text *Der Hungerpastor*, Delius berates Raabe for employing weather symbolism as an easy shorthand for thicker realistic description and for ignoring those "die noch im vom Kapitalismus produzierten Dreck stehen" (Delius 1971, 50). The disagreeable screed is interested not in literature but in the pretense of employing intellectual work as guerrilla warfare. How thin and pinched Delius's focus on *Der Hungerpastor* turns out to be appears in a colorful essay of 1986 on the multifarious literary echoes in Raabe's weather imagery by Eckhardt Meyer-Krentler, of whom there will be more to say presently.

A friendlier view is taken by Günter Matschke in what was originally a University of Oregon dissertation, published in 1975. Matschke, who agrees with Helmers (1968b, 13) that Raabe was a "Linksintellektueller" (Matschke 1975, 10), sees the isolation of his characters in a social-critical dimension. This is certainly just, though in my view he underestimates the tension and ambiguity of the late works when he sees them as developing "zu einem abgeklärteren, gereiften und humanen Konzept," figured in Stopfkuchen, who frees isolation from negativity and turns it into a worthwhile way of life (67). Of Stopfkuchen he remarks that "hinter dem äußerlich bürgerlichen Lebenstil … verbirgt sich seine innere Unbürgerlichkeit, seine Toleranz und geistige Beweglichkeit" (141), as though tolerance and flexibility were not historically bourgeois attributes.

In 1980 Matschke's somewhat naively affirmative view drew the fire of Uwe Heldt, who revived the topic of the idyll, but with a pejorative connotation. Heldt ascribes to Raabe's characters a desire for a life without alienation and therefore to Raabe an anti-capitalist intention, but without being able to cross the boundary of private property (Heldt 1980, 27). Of Stopfkuchen Heldt oddly claims that "sein Besitz ist ihm zugefallen, seine Existenz bleibt von Nicht-Arbeit geprägt" (28), when one of the main themes of

Stopfkuchen's monologue is the exceptional mental and physical labor that taking possession of the *Rote Schanze* has required. When Heldt fixes upon the idyllic spaces lost to capitalism in *Prinzessin Fisch* and *Pfisters Mühle* (69-70), his Marxism takes on a notably conservative coloration. He reads *Pfisters Mühle* against the grain, seeing Ebert not only as a limited but also as an ironically exposed narrator, whose acceptance of capitalist depradation cannot correspond to the author's (184-87). In general, however, Heldt sees Raabe as an ideologically blinded writer:

> Bürgerliche Kultur erscheint als der letzte Kitt, der eine ehmals starke und mit hohen Idealen angetretene Klasse zusammenhält: Freilich nur deren ideologischer Teil, das kleine Grüppchen der "Übriggebliebenen." Die reale gesellschaftlich-geschichtliche Potenz der Bourgeoisie, der Kapitalismus, tritt bei Raabe als blindes Fatum, als gleichförmig ablaufendes historisches Prozessieren auf. (223)

In one place Heldt rather provocatively observes that both Raabe and Nietzsche reflect the threat of the proletarization of the petty bourgeoisie by capitalism and that it is thus understandable that both became heroes of fascism (138).

This and other efforts have shown that the Western neo-Marxist approach has not been very fruitful. Gernot Folkers begins his 1976 study of the bourgeois illusion of property and security in Goethe and Raabe with the observation that people buy insurance as a commodity because they lack communal solidarity (Folkers 1976, 1), and it pretty much goes on in this inane style. Folkers argues that, of the late nineteenth-century German writers, only Raabe never separated petty-bourgeois resignation from the reality of the disappearance of the resources from which the bourgeoisie had drawn its strength, even though he could not see the proletarian solution (5-6). Wunnigel's fascination with antiques is a latent, anti-capitalist longing for a different society, though futile because retrograde and consumption-oriented; to show this could not, of course, have been Raabe's intention (90). The works of the 1880s express the hopelessness within the capitalist system (97). When Velten Andres in *Die Akten des Vogelsangs* burns his mother's possessions, he "ist zu einem Schauspieler in einer Tragödie geworden, deren Autor das Kapital ist" (120). Only proletarian solidarity can rescue the future (129), etc.

In 1980 an even more orthodox, true-believing Marxist, Walter Schedlinsky, published a study of Raabe's relationship to what he called the "industriegesellschaftliche Entwicklung." The only industry to which he gives much attention is publishing, from the point of view of the isolation of the writer under capitalist conditions from his public and his consequent alienation and identity problem, figured first of all in the narrator of the *Chronik*, himself an ideologically distorted and alienated personality. The class relations in *Die Leute aus dem Walde* are opaque to the narration itself; only the modern critic can interpret them. Schedlinsky finds in this novel an early symptom of the importation of "die amerikanische Ideologie vom 'self-made man'" (Schedlinsky 1980, 245); Eva, however, recognizes the heartless, loveless tendencies of American society at once (261). Schedlinsky sees the erotic dimension of *Unruhige Gäste*, in its dialectic with religious repression, more clearly than most commentators, but on the whole he is inclined, mistakenly, I believe, to see Veit as a potential liberator of the repressed Phöbe; here it is possible that Raabe's sensitivity to class consciousness is subtler than Schedlinsky's. Nevertheless, in my judgment the treatment of *Unruhige Gäste* is the best part of the study, even if it keeps reverting to such doctrinal equivocations as the claim that Valerie's possession of Veit reflects Marx's view of the dominance of man by man under capitalism (434). Fortunately, not too many doctoral candidates like these chose Raabe as a topic.

Similarly, although the neo-Marxist development in German scholarship came to have considerable influence on English-speaking Germanists, the English-language Raabe critics do not prominently exhibit this effect. One who does is the then English, now Floridian scholar Keith Bullivant. In 1976 he argued that Raabe was an exception to the naive social affirmativeness of the German realists by breaking with the focus on the individual evaluated by his degree of integration with the society; he did so primarily with the reminiscence technique (Pascal) of the first-person narrations, which "lack an omniscient, third-person narrator, they have no straighforward chronology and none of the sense of teleology that one finds in novels asserting the autonomy of the individual" (Bullivant 1976, 271). Almost a decade later he took up the same topic, this time in a German-language essay, in which he argues that German social conditions did not permit the style of the European novel and that Raabe's subjective narrator and problematic protagonist was the only possibility of breaking with idealist aesthetics and "das die Autonomie des Individuums verkündende Teleologische" (Bullivant 1984, 12).

b: The Modern and the (?) Post-Modern

Slowly and sporadically, some of the preoccupations of contemporary criticism have begun to touch the margins of Raabe study. From time to time there have been psychological forays into his texts, even though they have seemed rather resistant to them owing to their narrative mannerisms, which both puppetize characters and veil the narrator with his own garrulousness. It was not until 1976 that a systematic psychoanalytic study was undertaken by Paul Derks, focused primarily on *Stopfkuchen* and *Das Odfeld*. Derks wishes to break with the tradition of seeing Stopfkuchen as a hero; his interpretation turns on his understanding of Stopfkuchen's revelation of the secret of the killing of Kienbaum as "ein Akt offener Aggression" (Derks 1976, 13), a reading with which I fully agree. He charges Stopfkuchen with blindness to his own motives and class bias. In this part of the study, Derks, who takes Freud's analysis of Wilhelm Jensen's *Gradiva* as a model, is not attempting to psychoanalyze the author but to provide a psychogram of the narrators Eduard and Stopfkuchen in their repressed, hostile interaction with one another. Eduard's mention of Platen causes Derks to dilate at considerable length on the Heine-Platen conflict and the issue of homosexuality as a subtext. Much of this is interesting, though many of the other more or less subliminal echoes Derks finds in the text seem to me a little farfetched.

With *Das Odfeld* he reverses his procedure; here he seeks to psychoanalyze Raabe himself by interpreting the battle of the ravens, which has long intrigued and baffled critics. Derks elaborately traces the raven image through its many occurrences and rightly, it seems to me, regards it as a shifting, subtle metonymy for the author himself, though when he finds in the raven battle, because it is a fight among birds of the same species, repressed homosexual tendencies in the author, I am inclined to be skeptical. In any case, I tend to prefer my own, more inner-literary interpretation of the development of the raven image and its employment in *Das*

Odfeld (Sammons 1985b). I am quite sure that I do not believe Rainer Noltenius's psychosocial reading of the poem Raabe recited at the Schiller Centennial in Wolfenbüttel, since it brings such heavy artillery to bear on a youthful piece of patriotic bombast and comes to conclusions about Raabe's psychic disposition quite contrary to my own observations (Noltenius 1984, 113-43).

The perhaps inevitable amalgam of socio-psychoanalysis with critical sociology, poststructuralism, and discourse analysis has been formed in a difficult monograph of 1988 by Irmgard Roebling, who calls upon, among others, Lacan, Kristeva, and Kittler as well as Adorno, Benjamin, Bloch, Bachofen, and Marx. She denominates the mature Raabe's novel form as the *Spaltungsroman*, which articulates and structurally reflects the *fin-de-siècle* crisis of bourgeois individuality and subverts the symbolic-paternal discourse of authority, repression, and property with a semiotic-maternal discourse of nurturing tolerance and resistance to industry, capitalism, and progress. I must confess to not having understood all of this, but I find the postulated crisis of the bourgeois consciousness exaggerated, both in general and in Raabe's case, and I think the interpretive results very mixed. They are sometimes intriguing, regarding, for example, *Zum wilden Mann*, sometimes tendentious and distortive, for example, when Velten is made to represent the nurturing, maternal principle in *Die Akten des Vogelsangs*. It is interesting that Roebling's feminism is not a matter of emancipation, but rather of the predication to the maternal and the matriarchal positively valued qualities of peaceableness, nurturing, lovingness, organicism, closeness to nature, indifference to achievement and property, harmony, anarchy, primitive communism, and sensual reason. To my mind there is a question whether the undeniable romanticism of this complex does not run some risk of becoming reactionary. Whether Roebling's ambitious initiative is a harbinger of further deconstructive or post-modern exercises on Raabe remains to be seen. I cannot say that I altogether welcome the prospect, but others may.

Roebling's feminist aspect, such as it may be, is one of the unusual features of her effort. Raabe has doubtlessly not looked like a very fruitful topic for feminist inquiry, though here, too, one might discover that curious split between the conventionality of his opinions and the more liberated imaginativeness of his figurations. The major study of his representation of women, leaving aside the unpublished dissertation of Graves, is a 1981 monograph by Margrit Bröhan, which examines the female characters primarily in Stuttgart works: *Die Gänse von Bützow, Abu Telfan, Der Schüdderump,* and *Der Dräumling.* Before this, she argues, Raabe's women are loyal, passive, and timid (Bröhan 1981, 55), a claim that overlooks a number of forceful and independent female characters, some of whom she then mentions in the course of the discussion. She does comment on Raabe's early *femmes fatales* and the literary history behind them; to my mind they belong to his most melodramatic and least persuasive creations. She has worthwhile things to say about the diminished and isolated fate of the women in *Abu Telfan,* particularly in regard to criticism's often misplaced admiration for Klaudine as a wise woman (esp. 147-48, 152), and about the way in which Adelheid's alertness to prevent a *mésalliance* and her subdued but active class prejudice contribute to the tragedy of *Der Schüdderump* (171-78). The extent to which Bröhan keys Raabe's representations of women to the evolution of the liberal, bourgeois women's movement in the nineteenth century seems to me somewhat questionable, but, as Irene Di Maio has pointed out, there is more to be done on this front, both in interpretation and reception history (Di Maio 1981a), and Bröhan's work provides an impetus for further study.

A new development, if not post-modern, then certainly post-Marxist, is the reopening of the religious dimension of Raabe's writing by Heinrich Detering in a difficult and original monograph of 1990. Religion is an old but somewhat discredited topic in Raabe criticism. Perhaps owing to the indispensable presence of clergymen as part of the petty-bourgeois constellation of the cult, there was a tendency to present him as an affirmer of Christian values and a writer of religious feeling *quand même,* despite his not infrequent displays of religious indifference in his life and the critique of intolerance, the absence of Christian referents, and the wholly secular and skeptical perspective in the works, even those that take place in a realm of belief or contain clerical characters. Detering reopens the question in a modern way by examining not the beliefs of the empirical author but the narrative structures. What he finds is a continuous, multiperspectival, highly stressed engagement with the ultimate eschatological questions, which in its pronounced skepticism of poetic justice, its grim refusal of redemptive hope and the social and historical experience of the *deus absconditus*, can be understood, if not religiously, in some sense theologically insofar as it parallels modern ideas of a radical, disillusioned, negative theology, above all that of Barth and Kierkegaard. Detering recognizes a recurrent motif of *imitatio Christi* in the suffering and compassion of exemplary characters, who create religious meaning in a world otherwise bereft of religion and God. I am too unfamiliar with this context to have a very useful opinion about it. But Detering's study presents a series of stimulating, indeed engrossing interpretations: of *Zum wilden Mann* as a story of a pact with the devil; of *Unruhige Gäste*, where he counterpoints the often discussed biblical referents to the less noticed secular allusions to Shakespeare's *Much Ado about Nothing*; of Raabe's reading in Bible criticism and alternative views of the historical Jesus as they affect *Im alten Eisen*; of the metaphor of the Flood in *Höxter und Corvey, Das Odfeld*, and *Stopfkuchen*; of the ambiguous *imitatio Christi* of Velten Andres in *Die Akten des Vogelsangs*; of the replacement of theodicy with willed poetic illusion in *Hastenbeck*; of the breakdown not only of the answers but also of the questions in *Altershausen*. This brilliant book won a prize of the Raabe-Gesellschaft, and rightly so. It is one of the most probing, observant, and at the same time independent studies of Raabe ever written; any seriously comprehensive Raabe criticism of the future will have to weigh it thoughtfully and patiently.

The considerable amount of discourse about Raabe's representation of and attitude toward the Jews might also be treated in this place, for it is a both significant and exemplary aspect of the modern critical development. However, I believe it is more efficiently discussed in connection with the critical history of *Der Hungerpastor*, so it will be postponed to the next chapter.

In what has come to look like a post-Marxist phase, there have been signs of a new formalism. One impressive example is Wieland Zirbs, *Strukturen des Erzählens: Studien zum Spätwerk Wilhelm Raabes*, originally a Munich dissertation. Zirbs defines the *Spätwerk* as beginning after 1880; *Else von der Tanne, Meister Autor, Zum wilden Mann*, and even *Alte Nester* are transitional to the late phase (Zirbs 1986, 32-33). He sees the late Raabe as distinctly proto-modern, carrying the tradition of Sterne, Jean Paul, and Karl

Immermann into the language skepticism and bifurcation of reality and imagination characteristic of the modern. Fiction is redoubled, a construction pyramided on a subjectively perceived reality (67). Zirbs's "anthropological" approach operates with the dichotomies of oral versus written discourse and monologue versus dialogue. There are many fine interpretive insights, for example, a parallel of the failure to grasp reality in *Altershausen* with Feyerabend's failure to achieve his purpose as well as with the breakdown of the novel itself (118); a good discussion of the internalization of the subjective protagonist by the third-person narrator in *Else von der Tanne* (121-27); and the identification of *Meister Autor* as the first fully developed case of the solitary, monologuing narrator (158). On the whole, however, I found this study quite difficult and thought it might be excessively abstract and oversubtle in its insistence on proto-modernism.

An unclassifiable figure among contemporary German literary scholars is Eckhardt Meyer-Krentler, whose stupendous memory for texts, associative ingenuity, and engaging style are capable of nearly persuading the reader of contextual interpretations that one would otherwise have thought hardly plausible. This is the case with his monograph on *Der Lar* of 1986. In dense detail he treats the text as a puzzle to be solved, finding all sorts of unexpected satirical, primarily literary allusions. Identifying, correctly, I expect, the corpse-photographer and pornographer Blech as a homosexual, Meyer-Krentler claims that the novel is a hidden attack on Raabe's editor Adolf Glaser, who had been charged with pederasty some ten years before. In order to maintain his position, Meyer-Krentler must argue that Rosine Müller, far from being a positive figure, is a shallow chatterbox standing in for the trivial reader Raabe is combatting, and that Schnarrwergk's temporarily incapacitating stroke, which provides the opportunity for his nephew Paul and Rosine to fall in love with one another, is a crafty sham to lure them into an unhappy marriage. Any reader of *Der Lar* will be not a little astonished at this sinister interpretation, which I do not think can be accepted no matter how lawyerly the argument. But some of the details are compelling, and Meyer-Krentler's ingenuity has the virtue of calling attention to the still undiscovered layers of sometimes rascally allusiveness in Raabe's texts.

As any interpreter of *Der Lar* must, Meyer-Krentler raises the question of the influence of Darwinism. In fact, with his customary contrariness, he depicts Paul as a case of reverse Darwinism, the survival of the stupidest (Meyer-Krentler 1986b, 58). Raabe's interest in Darwinism, which has been touched upon from time to time, has been given an elaborate treatment in a long, learned article by Eberhard Rhose in the 1988 *Raabe-Jahrbuch*. Rohse demonstrates an ongoing response to the Darwinian controversy in Raabe's texts beginning as early as the Stuttgart period, and a lively interest in the German evolutionists, particularly Ernst Haeckel. Rohse's discussion extends well beyond my own competence in these matters; it proves, however, that Raabe, whose fiction is less overtly philosophical than that of many other German writers, was alertly attentive to the contemporary front line of progressive intellectual discourse and was far from the introverted, provincial ruminator he is often taken to be.

c: A New Empiricism

One of the recurrent characteristics of the sometimes nearly unbearable sophistication of today's literary criticism is a rather condescending view of the "positivism" of the past; even if it is acknowledged to have laid the foundation of everything we know and makes our work possible, it is thought to be antiquated and, at any rate, finished once and for all. But this is not the case; it is surprising how much of the foundation work, especially in biography and philology, has had to be redone. For empirical answers, like any others, are shaped by the questions asked, by the *Erkenntnisinteresse* that impels them. This has turned out to be true of Raabe, despite the vast intimacy of the cultists of the past with the materials and the often trivial details they brought to light.

The most productive of the scholar-researchers reexamining the *Realia* has been the prominent Berlin Germanist Horst Denkler. He has participated in the modern discussion at many points. Before the Raabe-Gesellschaft itself he spoke unmincingly of its seriously compromised past, also calling for new basic editorial work on the texts, the letters, and the unpublished biographical and reception materials (Denkler 1987a). As we shall see in the next chapter, he has participated vigorously in the discussion about Raabe's relationship to the Jews. He has encouraged the ecological interest in *Pfisters Mühle,* a matter he must regard as important, as he has recurred to it four times (Denkler 1980a; 1980b, 225-51; 1981; 1988a, 81-102). Above all he has made a point of returning to the archival materials, not only the diary, which most scholars have consulted, but also the unpublished correspondence, the notebooks, and documents of his life such as the household account books. In 1988 he collected ten of his studies into a volume (Denkler 1988a). Along with the ecological appropriation of *Pfisters Mühle,* the discussions of the Jewish problem, and studies of Raabe's relationship to Braunschweig (Denkler 1986b) and Berlin (Denkler 1988b), the most controversial item is a strong claim for the disruption in Raabe's life and writing caused by his erotic attraction to his best friend's wife, Marie Jensen (Denkler 1986a), while one of the most interesting is a revelation of Arno Schmidt's typically idiosyncratic fascination with Raabe (Denkler 1985).

It was apparent that these studies were preparatory to a new biographical effort, published in the following year (Denkler 1989b). Denkler conspicuously avoids the traditional "life and works" structure, perhaps to indicate a belief that it is no longer tenable in the midst of the epistemological skepticism of modern criticism. He begins with the material relics of Raabe's life and then launches in some detail into the reception history; only then does he turn, briefly, to a chronological account of the uneventful life, after which treats in more detail the family background, Raabe's marriage, his daily life, finances, erotic feelings, sociability, religious views (such as they may be), politics and working habits; here he reasserts his thesis concerning Marie Jensen without necessarily proving it. In the third part Denkler takes up the work of interpretation, at first concentrating unexpectedly on a brief, peripheral, and little respected sketch of 1884, *Der Besuch,* then attempting to characterize the œuvre as a whole by defining its themes and motifs, its socio-political involvements and communicative intentions, its allusiveness, structure, and narrative variety. Naturally there is much one might wish to dispute in both the strategy and the execution of this work, but it is a product of industrious research combined with careful thought attuned to the most modern concerns, and is therefore one of the indispensable contributions to current criticism. It is not, however, a book for the uninformed, for it presupposes a thorough acquaintance with Raabe's texts. It therefore cannot be a first resource for learning, as the more traditional form of biography could be, so that for that role we still have no modern successor to the contaminated work of Fehse.

Denkler is, of course, not the only one who engages in empirical research; biographical, contextual, and reception-historical materials of varying interest appear constantly. One of the most valuable is Jochen Meyer's detailed and engagingly illustrated chronicle of Raabe's years in Stuttgart, published under the aegis of the *Deutsches Literaturarchiv* in Marbach (Meyer, J. 1981). It probably gives the clearest, most realistic picture we have of Raabe's literary and political context in Stuttgart, in which he placed such great hopes, made such good friends, and was eventually so disappointed. Another quasi-biographical publication is a guidebook to the Weser River hill country setting of much of Raabe's fiction (Göhmann and Göhmann 1979). This may seem to fall out of the realm of criticism, but for anyone who is not native to the territory it is a useful vade mecum. I found that it contributed to the illumination I gained from visiting the locales and the landscape that were ever in Raabe's imagination.

Another aid for which researchers have reason to be grateful is a catalogue of the Raabe holdings of the archives in Braunschweig, including the Technical University, the Duke August Library in Wolfenbüttel, and the *Deutsches Literaturarchiv* in Marbach (Garzmann and Schuegraf 1985). It replaces another, less complete catalogue (Daum and Schuegraf 1981) that was unpublished but available to researchers in the Braunschweig Municipal Library. The new edition is a basic bibliographic resource for any systematic Raabe researcher. Denkler is present here as well, with an essay on some of the insights that can be gained from the archival material.

6: Criticism of Individual Texts: Some Examples

OUR EFFORT TO FOLLOW THE EVOLUTION of Raabe criticism more or less chronologically has tended to highlight comprehensive treatments while adducing interpretations of individual texts as exemplary for the larger development. Naturally, however, a large proportion of the criticism is focused on individual texts, and some attention to that dimension seems necessary to fill out the picture. It is a little difficult to know how best to go about this. Raabe wrote altogether sixty-eight works of fiction. Most of them have some critical history, though the extent and the continuity into the present vary greatly. Tracing how once popular texts fade from critical discourse, while previously neglected ones have blossomed, would be a possible way of delineating the development. One of sociological significance would be to follow the reception and analysis of the historical fiction. Another would be to pick texts that have recurrently been the object of attention, such as the *Chronik, Pfisters Mühle, Prinzessin Fisch,* or *Altershausen,* or alternatively, those that have presented interpretive puzzles owing to their untypical features, such as *Altershausen* again, *Die Innerste,* or *Vom alten Proteus.* Without prejudice to any of these possibilities, I have elected to sketch the critical response to works that, by common consent, belong to any literary-historical canon of Raabe's œuvre: the informally designated Stuttgart and Braunschweig "trilogies," and, as outstanding examples of the shorter prose, the linked stories *Zum wilden Mann* and *Unruhige Gäste.*

a: The Stuttgart Trilogy

The three ambitious novels that came to be known as the Stuttgart trilogy — *Der Hungerpastor, Abu Telfan,* and *Der Schüdderump* — mark a kind of watershed in Raabe's career. With them he strained every resource to establish himself with the public as a major writer. His failure to do so led to his irrevocably embittered estrangement from the public; it also turned him away from novel writing itself for a number of years, as he returned to stories and novellas, not least for reasons of economic advantage. It is a redoubled irony that the first of these books, *Der Hungerpastor*, which, like the others, had a slow start, eventually came the closest to realizing his desires and, in consequence, turned into the major stumbling block for the rehabilitation of his reputation. *Der Hungerpastor* came to be his most canonical book, as he himself, with some misgivings, was obliged to recognize. It is the title that everyone who knows one thing about him associates with him, and to no small extent his reputation rose and fell with the critical apprehension of it.

The discussion of *Der Hungerpastor* has been preoccupied with two main concerns: the implications of the figuration of the sinister Jewish intellectual Moses Freudenstein, alias, after his opportunistic conversion to Catholicism, Théophile Stein, and, by extension, Raabe's attitude to the Jews; and the related question of whether and to what extent the novel is modelled on Gustav Freytag's huge best seller of 1855, *Soll und Haben*, perceived, perhaps not altogether precisely, as the most explicitly anti-Semitic of the commonly known German literary works of the nineteenth century. The matter is complicated by the fact that, during the pre-fascist and Nazi phases of Raabe's reputation, his novel was praised as healthily anti-Semitic and offered as main evidence for appropriating him as precursor of National Socialism. While it is, as always, difficult to gauge the motives of hundreds of thousands of readers, it is not implausible that the novel appeared to reassure some substantial number of them in their Judeophobic affects, as is likely also the case with the nearly century-long popularity of *Soll und Haben*.

Discussion of the implications of Jewish characterization in *Der Hungerpastor* has accompanied the whole history of Raabe criticism; in fact, it began during his lifetime (see Sammons 1987, 82-83). As I have pointed out earlier (see above, p. 14), an essay published by Josef Bass immediately after Raabe's death surveyed his Jewish characterizations positively. But not everyone was persuaded by such arguments. E. K. Bramsted, in his pioneering sociological study of the German novel (originally published in

1937), called them "whitewashing" and insisted that Freudenstein was meant as a typical Jewish figure, not as a renegade, as Raabe, and others following him, asserted (Bramsted 1964, 148). This view has been widely held and for many scholars and intellectuals erected a barrier to closer acquaintance with the author. The relationship of the novel to _Soll und Haben_ has also been diversely viewed. The cultists, it seems to me, did not pursue the question very actively. The American Walter Silz broached it in 1924, as I have mentioned (see above, pp. 47-48). In Pongs we find the oddity that in his monograph he dismisses it, claiming that the resemblance is only a matter of "grobe Umrisse" (Pongs 1958, 215), while in his commentary to the _Der Hungerpastor_ in the Braunschweig edition he takes it as a given (6: 469). He is otherwise insistent that Freudenstein does not stand for the Jewish people, noting that he is repudiated by the other Jews in the novel (Pongs 1958, 219).

Over the years there have been a number of ways of dealing with these problems and with the novel in general. In 1969 Marketa Goetz-Stankiewicz took an original tack by proposing that Freudenstein is one of Raabe's fictionalized partial alter egos, that he represents his struggle from convention and one pole of his duality (Goetz-Stankiewicz 1969, 28-31). Four years later some support came from a judicious French study of Jewish figures in German literature. While arguing that Raabe saw the Jews as products of a new economic order he detested and as in all cases different in character from gentiles, the author compares him favorably with Freytag as more empathic and understanding, and denies that he was anti-Semitic (Angel 1973, 23-24, 182-85). Responding to this in part, a treatment of _Der Hungerpastor_ as a _Pfarrerroman_ without religion takes Freudenstein to be a Mephisto figure in a Faustian drama (Mohr 1977, 62), which may not help us much, as the passive, morally sensitive Hans Unwirrsch is not a very Faustian character. More recently, Hans Otto Horch, one of today's foremost experts on German-Jewish literary relations, again denies that Freudenstein was a representative Jew or that Raabe was in any way anti-Semitic (Horch 1985, 165); he defends Freytag against the charge of anti-Semitism also.

There have been various efforts to move the discussion away from these concerns. Daemmrich, for example, treats the work objectively and descriptively as one of the "novels of development" (Daemmrich 1981, 79-84). Others have looked at it as a type of *Bildungsroman*. Monica Weber Clyde sees it, like *Die Leute aus dem Walde*, in succession to Goethe's *Wilhelm Meister*, but with the decisive change that characters are fixed by preconceived laws and not free to develop, so that *Bildung* in its Goethean sense is put into question or displaced by practical, common-sensical wisdom (Clyde 1968, 45, 65). Gerhart Mayer has come to similar conclusions. While he sees *Der Hungerpastor* as Raabe's only *Bildungsroman* — *Die Leute aus dem Walde* he denominates an *Erziehungsroman* — he too finds no development in Hans other than a discovery through disillusionment of his own inwardness (Mayer, G. 1980, 101, 106-07). This inward movement is exactly contrary to that of *Soll und Haben*, which leads toward accultura-tion and social affirmation (105). This point I think well taken.

None of this discussion suggests that *Der Hungerpastor* is likely to be restored to its premier position of the past. Most contem-porary commentary is critical or dismissive. Jörg Thunecke, for example, has compared Raabe's handling of his Jewish themes quite unfavorably to that of George Eliot in *Daniel Deronda* (Thunecke 1987). Rudi Schweikert has focused on what I believe to be one of the novel's most damaging infelicities: the superinten-ding metaphor of hunger in its formulaic repetitiveness, its blatant purpose of manipulating reader response, and its incoherence (Schweikert 1978). Friedrich Sengle, on the other hand, eschews evaluation from a modern standpoint by attempting to maintain a rigorously literary-historical view, characteristically locking the novel into his inclusive category of *Biedermeier*, though surely as one of its latest phenomena. He does not doubt the modelling influence of *Soll und Haben* or that Raabe was attempting thereby to accommodate himself to his public (Sengle 1981, 84). Raabe's subjective narration, he argues, does not presage modernism but harks back to Romanticism (82), though I cannot see why it cannot do both. On the Jewish problem Sengle is somewhat eclectic. In Freudenstein he sees Raabe's rejection of Young German liberal writing oriented on Paris; following Goetz-Stankiewicz, he interprets Freudenstein as a projection of part of the author's own personality, and, like others before him, as untypical of Jewishness; and while he acknowledges an element of what he calls literary anti-Semitism, he insists that it should not be linked to the fate of the Jews leading up to the Holocaust (84-86).

Since the early 1980s the discussion has again veered away from focus on the novel to more general assessments of Raabe's overall characterization of Jews, in which Freudenstein appears as an anomaly for which the contrite author tried to compensate in other works, and to the reasonably decent though not spotless attitude toward and relations with Jews in his personal life (Arendt 1980b; Sammons 1986; Denkler 1984, 1987b, 1989a). Denkler's 1987 article in the *German Quarterly* drew some acerbic comment from those who found his defense of Raabe apologetic and insensitive (Holub 1987; Nägele 1988). While these critiques did not seem to be founded in a full awareness of the dimensions of Raabe's discourse on the Jews, in retrospect I have come to think that the expositions of it, including my own, do suffer from a desire to put Raabe in the best possible light, glossing over some of the less agreeable evidence, and failing above all to put him into the context of the scientific discourse on race of the time, in which he showed considerable interest. It is unlikely, therefore, that the discussion is at an end.

Among critics, if not among readers, the second novel of the trilogy, *Abu Telfan*, has come to displace *Der Hungerpastor* as an object of interest. There can be no doubt that this is owing to its thrust of social and political criticism, which is present in *Der Hungerpastor*, but sporadically, whereas in *Abu Telfan* it is thematic. That the socio-political dimension is the initial stimulant was demonstrated in a quite unexpected way in 1980, when the venerable Marxist Hans Mayer nominated *Abu Telfan* for a list of the one hundred best books being compiled by the weekly *Die Zeit* (Mayer, H. 1980). Not long afterwards, and probably virtually simultaneously, the East German Hans Kolbe also gave the novel a respectful treatment in this light (Kolbe 1981a, 28-52).

Nevertheless, attentive reading has always made it difficult to sustain this view unequivocally. Kolbe himself is obliged to observe that, after Hagebucher's one act of rebellion, in his lecture to the community, he no longer develops (44), and he is obliged to fall back on the novel's utopian hope rather than figuration of the ultimate humane victory (42-43). Daemmrich sees the social criticism in the novel as lacking any solution (Daemmrich 1981, 84-85). Long before, Barker Fairley had dismissed it as a bungle, an evasion of its own socio-political implications (Fairley 1961, 166-68). The reasons for this will be evident to any reader. The novel contains the most notorious praise of philistinism in Raabe's works (7: 357-58). The protagonist Hagebucher, who seems to have become alienated from his own society through his ten years of slavery in Africa, comes to an accommodation with it, lives as a rentier served by his mother and sister, and comes physically to resemble the father who had disowned him. There is a vast amount of praise, not only by the characters but also on the narrative level, of Klaudine von Fehleysen, Our Lady of Patience, a very icon of passivity, who ends, along with the defeated rebellious female figure, Nikola, in a life of total stasis. While early critics tended to identify Klaudine with the ethos of the novel and accepted her denomination as a wise woman, more recent observers have been disturbed by her and her role (see, for example, Meinerts 1940, 196, n. 14; Graves 1978, 149; Bröhan 1981, 147-48). Furthermore, the apparent course of the novel appears to be distracted by elements drawn from conventional fiction that may seem, in this context, somewhat meretricious (Reece 1975, 209).

The most precise observations on the difficulty have been made, in my opinion, by Stephen A. Gould. He sees the narrator at the outset as distinct from and superior to Hagebucher; the social criticism is on the narrator's account, not Hagebucher's (Gould 1976, 179). He, too, complains that, despite the revolutionary rhetoric of some of the characters, especially Lieutenant Kind, the novel is unwilling "to propound revolutionary social action" (180). He finds a confusion of voice: "the rhetorical support of the von Fehleysen variation conflicts with the support of the Hagebucher episodes and thus contributes negatively to the rhetorical structure of the work as a whole" (181). He sees a contradiction between the praise afforded Klaudine and the actual bad consequences of her advice, which contributes to several disasters, including Hagebucher's catastrophic lecture (185). The narrator's need to support both Klaudine and Hagebucher against the logic of his own story leads, in Gould's view, to a disappearance of irony from the narration (186).

It is primarily Gould's analysis that lies behind my own criticism of *Abu Telfan* as irresolute in form (Sammons 1987, 213-16). However, I tried to show that the novel is not so much a bungle as an effort to cope in integrity with incompatible commitments; if it is ultimately incoherent, the incoherence is in itself significant and interpretable, and, despite it, there are strengths in the book, including its satirical-critical promise, that make it deserving of the regard in which it has come to be held. A more recent discussion equates the figure of the returnee, of which Hagebucher is the prime example, with that of the *Sonderling* as a vehicle of social criticism, argues that the novel is sociologically congruent in that the simultaneity of oppressive stasis and insecurity is a mark of nineteenth-century society, and that the foreign and the *Heimat* have come to be interchangeable in the modern world, so that *Heimat* becomes a utopian vision rather than a realistically described category (Brenner 1989).

Abu Telfan has occasionally been employed for illustrative purposes. Hermann Helmers used the revisions of the fourth chapter between the magazine version and the book version in order to analyze characteristics of Raabe's often idiosyncratic language (Helmers 1962). A few years later an "ethnographic" interpretation was offered as an exemplary critique of critical method (Bachmann 1979). However, I am prevented from reporting on it as I was unable to understand it. Others better equipped methodologically may find it valuable. Finally, a welcome by-product of research into *Abu Telfan* has been the unearthing of Raabe's Stuttgart acquaintance Albert Dulk (1819-84), a radical freethinker and revolutionary activist who lived with three wives simultaneously and in later years was jailed as a Social Democrat; as a returnee in 1850 from an effort to live as a hermit in the Sinai he is thought to be a model for Hagebucher (see Meyer 1988). More important, however, is that the fervid petty-bourgeois Raabe obviously enjoyed the company of this truly spectacular and (unlike Hagebucher) incorrigible non-conformist.

In contrast to *Abu Telfan*, the third novel of the trilogy, *Der Schüdderump*, seems to have been gradually declining in critical interest. It is the darkest of all of Raabe's major works, the narrative machinery of which seems designed to frustrate readers' expectations of poetic justice. In the past, as a chief exhibit of Raabe's "pessimism," it met the fascination of the critics with Schopenhauer. This preoccupation has much diminished. In the early 1950s it was pointed out that Schopenhauer associated true love with pity, while in the novel Antonie sees Hennig's love as confused with pity and therefore rejects it (Neumann 1951/52, 325). The point was reiterated by Pongs (1958, 286). To be sure, the apparent relentlessness has been taken as a prefiguration of Naturalism and of the "illusionslose Schärfe der Moderne" (Klein 1968, 8).

What has made contemporary critics more uneasy is Raabe's rather heavy-handed management of the superintending metaphor, the death-cart, which is, in a sense, the opposite of an objective correlative, since it has no existence in the narrated story but rumbles about exclusively on the narrational plane. Fairley (1961, 180) was one of the first to find this device mismanaged. Hubert Ohl, worrying about it at a more sophisticated level, found contradictions in its symbolic application, on the one hand, as an allegory of a metaphysical force and, on the other, as an attribute of the temporally defined, specific evil of Dietrich Häussler (Ohl 1968, 83-84). More recently, Dieter Kafitz has commented on this that, although the overdetermination of the symbol

> führt zu einer Entkonkretisierung spezifischer gesellschaftlicher Gegebenheiten, andererseits tritt gerade dadurch die dem einzelnen undurchschaubar und unausweichlich erscheinende Bedrohung in gesteigerter Intensität hervor. (Kafitz 1978, 186)

As with *Abu Telfan*, efforts have been made to redirect interest to the novel's social-critical dimension. Daemmrich, for example, argues that it "expresses [Raabe's] skepticism of modern civilization and his passion for social justice most frankly"; it is a "broadside attack on a hateful system" in which values are undermined by the mercantile spirit (Daemmrich 1981, 88). The most elaborate argument of this kind was mounted, not surprisingly, by the East German Kolbe, for whom *Der Schüdderump* represents progress in recognition of economic determinants. For him Dietrich Häussler is the capitalist incarnate and his actions are an exemplary case of the destruction of humaneness by the "Besitzbürgertum" (Kolbe 1981b, 54). The well-meaning but tepid and ineffectual Hennig von Lauen, on the other hand, illustrates "das Versagen breiter Kreise des deutschen Bürgertums ..., das sich mit den gegebenen Verhältnissen und der reaktionären Entwicklung völlig abgefunden hat" (56). Strictly speaking, to be sure, Hennig belongs to the minor landed nobility, but Kolbe sees that as unimportant and the Lauen family as bourgeois in education and mentality (56). As is often the case with interpretations of this kind, it turns out that the author did not understand his own story; Raabe (partly through the image of the cart) falsely made timeless issues out of the historically temporary problems of bourgeois society (67-68).

The most positive view of *Der Schüdderump* among modern critics is, perhaps surprisingly, that of Gould. He sees in the novel a tragic structure reinforced by the narrator's deterministic insistence that evil cannot be blamed:

> By repeatedly declaring the question of guilt and innocence moot, the narrator directs the readers's attention away from individual personalities and a specific causality, to the two irreconcilable sets of value represented by the major characters. (Gould 1976, 199)

As for the cart, Gould does not find it employed capriciously:

> Except for its presence in the first five chapters where its symbolic connotations are developed, the cart appears only when events might lead the reader to anticipate Antonie's success in the temporal terms which the novel considers so superficial. (209)

This reading is connected with Gould's belief that the novel exhibits a "carefully constructed paradox of victory in defeat" (207). That Antonie's fate represents a moral victory on the ideal plane is, of course, an old idea. Neumann expressed it thus: "Das wahrhafte Glück dieser Welt liegt nicht in einem äußern Erfolg, sondern in der unsichtbaren Gemeinschaft derer, die 'aus dem tiefsten, reichsten Grunde der Welt' leben" (Neumann 1951/52, 325). That this was in general Raabe's view I do not doubt, but I do question whether it is effectively illustrated in this bleak, bitter novel. I am also a little at odds with Gould's defense of the cart. He rightly comments on the narrator's "animosity" to the reader in this novel and finds him "unusually authoritarian" (Gould 1976, 216, 218). My own view has been that the repeated running of the cart under the reader's nose is a reflex of this attitude, a symptom of the mistrust of the reader's ability to pay attention and get the meaning (Sammons 1987, 65).

b: The Braunschweig Trilogy

If, of the novels of the Stuttgart trilogy, the first has received the most attention, the case is the opposite with the Braunschweig trilogy; the first of the novels, *Alte Nester*, has been only intermittently discussed, even though it has been customary for critics, for example, Pongs (1958, 408) and Clyde (1968, 66), to see it as a turning point in Raabe's mature style. As with all the first-person narrations of the trilogy, much of the modern attention has been focused on the narrative level. Daemmrich (1981, 106) has remarked on the extent to which the narrator Langreuter dominates the story. Zirbs in particular has focused closely on the narrator, observing that he is primarily oriented on himself and is to be mistrusted when he claims otherwise (Zirbs 1986, 212). However, Langreuter is in some ways the most diminished in character of all of Raabe's major first-person narrators, and, though he is doubtless meant to attract our sympathy, his condition, crippled not only in body but in soul, petty, humorless, and timid, and so lacking in insight into the friends whose story he is telling that he does not realize until too late that Eva Sixtus had liked him, in my opinion has reduced the intensity and perhaps the reader's level of interest in the novel. Clyde sees Langreuter as a horrible example of conventional bourgeois *Bildung* with its flight into the idyllic (Clyde 1968, 88). Life and learning are now in opposition, and the concept of *Bildung*, or what it has become, is an object of criticism in the novel (70, 85-86). A more recent critic has interpreted it against the grain of what he takes to be Raabe's intention, arguing, as others have from time to time about various works, that it is a question whether the text shows what it appears to assert. The characters are more damaged by bourgeois society than Raabe admits (Schultz 1979, 136-37, 145).

The most likely new direction in interpretation of the novel has been adumbrated recently by Hans-Jürgen Schrader, who wants to break away from the analysis of the, in his view, thin, sketchy, and implausible plot, characterization, and message that preoccupies most of the discussion of *Alte Nester*, by seeing the object of the narration as narration itself and its theoretical reflection (Schrader 1989, 15). He argues that never before Thomas Mann's *Die Entstehung des Doktor Faustus* has there been a case of so much reflection on composition and reader response in a literary text (15). This is the by now familiar story of Raabe's resistance to the dominant doctrine of objective narration; Schrader reviews under several headings the means by which the conventional poetics of the novel are opened up to a self-aware literariness (24-26). Once again we are assured that Raabe points directly to literary modernism (27). However that may be, there seems to be little doubt that future criticism of *Alte Nester* will follow Schrader's lead.

In contrast to *Alte Nester*, the second novel of the three, *Stopfkuchen*, has been in the foreground of criticism. A case could be made that it has been the most important text in the modern discussion, that it has been the lever by which Raabe has been rescued from his "friends" and made accessible to contemporary interest. A full history of *Stopfkuchen* criticism would fill a book of this size, so that its lineaments can only be sketched here. While, like many of Raabe's best works, it was a relative failure with the public, it has always attracted the attention of connoisseurs, especially after it became apparent that Raabe himself had been uncharacteristically voluble about it, that he regarded it as his best work, and that he hinted that Stopfkuchen was in some sense an allegorical representation of himself (see Sammons 1987, 296-97). Herman Meyer called it

> eine runde und heile Schöpfung, ein Meisterwerk von europäischem Format, das sich neben klassischen humoristischen Romanen wie "Tristram Shandy" oder "Die toten Seelen" durchaus behauptet; (Helmers 1968a, 102)

Pongs asserted that it is "das einzige Raabesche Werk bisher, das unbezweifelt in den Rang der großen Romane der Weltliteratur aufgestiegen ist" (Pongs 1958, 552). It was the object of one of the earliest full monographs on Raabe, Hans Ahrbeck's of 1926. Ahrbeck, as the son-in-law of Raabe's close friend Edmund Sträter, was something of an insider, and his biographical interpretation, identifying Stopfkuchen with Raabe, who is denominated a "Lehrmeister der deutschen Nation" (Ahrbeck 1926, 24-25), and interpreting Stopfkuchen as a character who had made his life into a work of art (40), anticipated the terms of much of the discussion until relatively recently. Its modern history could be presented as a sequence of skeptical inquiries into the narrative technique, the reliability of the narrator Eduard, and the exemplary status of Stopfkuchen.

However, this development did not proceed in a straight line chronologically. There has been considerable diversity concerning the fundamental issues. To show this, we might look at three influential efforts. Hubert Ohl in 1964 opened the modern inquiry into the narrative technique, arguing that Stopfkuchen is riddling, disingenuous, hard to know, implicated in his own story, engaged in "Vexierung seines Zuhörers" (Eduard), against whom the whole performance is aimed as an act of vengeance, but with ambivalent results (Helmers 1968a, 249, 250, 252-53, 258, 261, 270). Peter Detroy's thoughtful, well argued monograph of 1970 follows upon Ohl by analyzing the shifting narrative time levels and also regards Stopfkuchen as ambiguous and still under stress, calling attention to the evolution of the image of the sloth, but ultimately he sees him as a positive figure who sublimates his aggressiveness and whose apparent ruthlessness is but a device to underline his points (Detroy 1970, 132-33). Unlike Ohl, he regards Eduard as a beneficiary of Stopfkuchen's treatment, as having been humanely educated to disillusion and to humor (49, 53, 88, 106-07, 115, 123). But in the same year the French scholar Claude David entered an objection against the modern valuation of the novel altogether, claiming that the narrative devices were merely tricky, that the narrator Eduard is of no interest, and that the work is a nihilistic humoresque that celebrates philistinism and comfortable withdrawal from the world's realities (David 1970, 263, 264, 268-74).

One might structure a reception history of the novel according to the ways interpreters pick their way among these possibilities. Gerhart Mayer, treating the work as a *Bildungsroman*, comes to a generally positive view of Stopfkuchen and a less positive one of Eduard (Mayer, G. 1980, 111-24). Daemmrich, on the other hand, rates Eduard more highly as a good listener and a superior, ironic narrator (Daemmrich 1979, 245). Clyde sees the reader set before a choice between Stopfkuchen or affirmation of conventional society, and Eduard as a dubious narrator implicated by Stopfkuchen in its conventionality; while Eduard self-ironizes his vanity, Stopfkuchen has achieved Humboldtian *Bildung* (Clyde 1968, 94, 99, 109, 113, 114, 122). Clyde has also analyzed the sloth motif, in connection with Schopenhauer (Clyde 1974), an association also taken up by Hans Dierkes, who links Schopenhauer with Stopfkuchen's capacity for *Anschauung*, while Eduard does not succeed in changing his life or transcending the temporal (Dierkes 1973, 94-95, 98, 104). Webster, reacting against Detroy and others, strives for evenhandedness, warning against idealization of Stopfkuchen as a successful raiser of consciousness and too dismissive a view of Eduard, whom he sees as a figure of some weight modifying Stopfkuchen's alleged superiority (Webster 1978, 156-57). Zirbs, however, sees Eduard subtly changing in the course of writing his memoir, but in the direction of self-protection and of weakening Stopfkuchen's effect on him (Zirbs 1986, 130-31, 192).

David, meanwhile, has undermined the confidence of others in the moral quality of the novel itself. In 1974 one of the admirers ventured the heresy that Stopfkuchen is egocentric, aggressive, ruthless and unforgiving in his campaign against Eduard, and demanding of praise (Schweckendiek 1974, 78-85). Stopfkuchen's philistinism is disturbing: "Der Ausdruck 'behagliche Weltverach- tung,' mit der Schaumann auf die Menschen der Kleinstadt 'herabblickt,' will mir nicht gefallen" (91), and he argues that Raabe, in his "Publikumsbeschimpfung" (94), forgot his own deterministic principle that no one is responsible for the way his psychobiology had formed him. Derks in his psychoanalytic study found that the ominous consequences for Störzer's family of Stopfkuchen's melodramatic exposure of him as the "murderer" merely per- petuate the injustice and insensitivity that Stopfkuchen claims to have transcended (Derks 1976, 9-23). More recently, Zirbs has located Stopfkuchen in a series of Narcissus figures, using language for self-representation and power (Zirbs 1986, 154).

This situation induced me to seek an interpretive solution that would take into account the insights of the ongoing discussion (Sammons 1987, 283-99, originally 1981). I sought to show that Eduard is an elusive narrator, trying to evade his own complicities and to change the meaning of the story Stopfkuchen tells him, but I wanted also to relieve the moral unease some observers have felt by questioning the exemplary status predicated to Stopfkuchen in older criticism and thus putting him at a distance from the author. Insofar as he represents Raabe, he does so parodistically and hyperbolically, and his campaign of vengeance is a failure because it "has struck a target that is too flaccid for it" (295). I suggest that there is wry comedy in the work, some of it directed by the author against himself.

Meanwhile, different perspectives on the work have emerged. Volkmar Sander found its modernity not only in the manipulation of narrative perspective, but also in the "Absage der sentimentalen Vergangenheitsbewältigung, die das geschichtsbesessene Jahrhundert hervorgebracht hat" (Sander 1968, 230). Brewster, unexpectedly but persuasively, brought out an anti-colonial dimension to the novel (Brewster 1983a). In 1979 Ulf Eisele tried to apply a structuralist technique to it, looking at Stopfkuchen as a detective, while Eduard is an incompetent detective, refuted by Stopfkuchen and condemned to write the story of his own blindness (Eisele 1979, 12-19). Eisele argues that Stopfkuchen's violent rhetoric, displaying language as a question of power, is not devised to punish Eduard, but to establish himself as an artist in bourgeois society (21, 32). The novel is an allegory of realism (56), and reflects the situation of the oppositional bourgeois writer who cannot join the working class (70). Mark Lehrer, agreeing with Brewster's anti-colonialist reading, discovered in the novel a parodistic reflex of Heinrich Schliemann's archaeological career, as well as a jab at his friend Jensen's admiration of Storm, which Raabe did not share (Lehrer 1989). This follows in part another typical tour de force of Meyer-Krentler, who sees the novel as a hostile parody of Storm's *Ein Doppelgänger* (Meyer-Krentler 1987). His reading is beguiling as always, difficult though it may be to believe that so intricate a novel was designed for such a relatively trivial purpose.

The discussion of the third novel, *Die Akten des Vogelsangs*, has gained momentum more slowly, but it has now reached comparable proportions as more observers come to the conclusion I share, that it may be, even more than *Stopfkuchen*, the finest achievement of Raabe's career. A strand of opposition to the conventional view sets in at a fairly early date and leads in a circuitous route to modern positions. The conventional view was of Velten Andres as a victor on the ideal plane, even if he failed in reality, and it made much of an alleged discipleship to Goethe. Relatively little attention was paid to the significance of the first-person narrator. Bönneken's early effort, which has been mentioned above (p. 27), made a special point of exaggerating the novel's hostility to America as a symbol of "Mammonismus" (Bön-neken 1926, 27, 97).

An early breakthrough in understanding came rather unexpec-tedly in a Göttingen dissertation by Hans Jürgen Meinerts published well into the Nazi period. The wretched printing of the book suggests that it appeared under what were already unpropitious circumstances. The intelligent, competent close reading is distinguished by its independence from authorities. Meinerts attacks the sainted Bönneken, criticizes the party line of the Raabe-Gesellschaft, and argues that the tone of the novel is more tragic than is suggested by Fehse (Meinerts 1940, 1, 197). He does, however, acknowledge a position of Fehse's that has re-mained fairly stable to the present: that the novel is in some sense an autobiographical meditation that reflects a split in the author's self (7; Fehse 1937, 566-67). Meinerts's strong point is his analytic attention to the narrator Krumhardt. He sees that Krumhardt in writing about the riddle of Velten seeks clarification about himself, and that it is just his insecurity that enables him to tell Velten's story (Meinerts 1940, 18, 44). He takes a critical view of Velten, showing that he tries to impose his world of perceptions upon others and is destroyed by trying to transfer dominance from the realm of imagination to reality (60-61). Unlike others who see Helene as a horrible example of Americanism, Meinerts acknow-ledges her will to assert herself (74). There are good observations on the dream world of the Des Beaux and Raabe's long maturation to a tragic sense. Though we would no longer agree with some of Meinerts's positions, such as that Velten is an incarnation of Schopenhauer's ideas or the surprising remark that the narrator is the least important of the characters (157), many of his themes have continued to be pertinent in the criticism of the novel.

Pongs, for example, argued quite reasonably that Raabe places Velten in a critical distance, while the narrator sees him too positively (Pongs 1958, 599-601). A 1972 paper finds the narrator in a "merkwürdiges Zwielicht" and senses his uneasiness in the shifts of time layers and disparities of time relationships, calculating that the narrator shifts between the frame and the inner story sixty times (Hahn, 1972, 61, 64). Webster dilated upon Krumhardt's insecurity and timidity about changing his own life (Webster 1979b, 241). Wolfgang Preisendanz, in a characteristically lucid and penetrating essay, which clearly owes something to Meinerts, writes of the narrator's dialogue with himself and his crisis of consciousness (Preisendanz 1981, 212-15, 220). Preisendanz warns against the occasionally adduced comparison of the novel with Thomas Mann's *Doktor Faustus* on the grounds that such a parallel would make Velten rather than Krumhardt the central figure (220; cf. also Zirbs 1986, 31, 217, and, on *Altershausen,* 231-32). While this point is well taken, I think a comparison in terms of narrative strategy is not without relevance. Nancy A. Kaiser has written of "the relativization of all possible positions," the "subtle undermining of the myth of the past idyllic community," the unreliability of Krumhardt as a narrator owing to the rigidity of his allegiances, the destabilization of "all representations of endurance," and "Velten's consistent refusal to become anyone other than himself, to integrate himself into a society whose priorities he does not share" as being "within the tradition of insistent middle-class individualism and self-determination" (Kaiser 1984, 3, 5, 7, 8). The French scholar Jean Royer has expanded learnedly on the signficance of the Des Beaux's Provençal origins (Royer 1987).

Of symptomatic importance is an essay published by Wilhelm Emrich in 1982, where he doubts that Velten is a victor, argues that Helene conducts herself as she does because she and her aspirations are disrespected in the Vogelsang, denies that the novel acts out a conflict between German *Gemüt* and American Mammonism, and locates Raabe firmly as a proto-modernist narrator (Emrich 1982, 12, 17-18, 21). These points, though relevant and well argued, are perhaps less significant than the appearance of the article itself, by one of the most prestigious of German literary scholars and a renowned interpreter of Goethe's *Faust*. It is compelling evidence for the successful academic recanonization of Raabe. Zirbs, though he does not cite Emrich, takes a comparable view of the novel's modernity; he sees Krumhardt, like Eduard in *Stopfkuchen,* changing in the course of writing, but in a more self-aware way (Zirbs 1986, 150-51).

As in the case of *Stopfkuchen,* there have been a number of innovative approaches to the text. A Jungian interpretation has been undertaken (Zwilgmeyer 1984). I would prefer not to comment on it, as I have never been able to comprehend the standard of verification in Jungian criticism; it seems to me, however, that some of the conclusions, such as Velten's role as a second soul demanding to be integrated by Krumhardt, could be reached without the Jungian apparatus. A perspective from the Left appeared in the Lensing/Peter volume. It accurately shows how Raabe especially with this novel broke with the program of harmonization and reintegration of experience of the Poetic Realism. When, however, it is argued that the Des Beaux represent a unified existence of the past and that their divergent courses in life represent the splitting of consciousness into capitalist endeavor and barren contemplativeness, and especially when it is claimed that Velten loses to capitalism's division of labor (Geisler 1981, 368, 370, 375-76), one may get the feeling that older views (e. g., about "Mammonism") are being recycled in new terminology. Irene Di Maio has shown how a number of feminist issues can be teased out of the text (Di Maio 1987). I have commented earlier on this aspect of Irmgard Roebling's effort (above, p. 95). For all its impressive dimensions, when she argues that Velten is actually liberating himself from his paternal, patriarchal heritage when he burns his mother's belongings and opens her house to looting (Roebling 1988, 160), then I think the text is being obliged to serve the system rather than vice versa.

c: The Harz Diptych

The above appellation is a facetious invention of my own. Raabe wrote a number of works set in the Harz region, including *Der Schüdderump*. But *Zum wilden Mann* and *Unruhige Gäste* are particularly interesting because they share the same setting and two overlapping characters, yet are very different in type, thus illuslustrating with particular precision the unusual variety of his modes of writing. *Zum wilden Mann* may remind us somewhat of E. T. A. Hoffmann, in that a story with fantastic elements is put into an almost pedantically realistic setting. Thoughts of fairy-tale motifs have recurred in the critical history (Butzmann 1949, 81-83; Daemmrich 1981, 97-98; Hoffmann 1986, 473). *Unruhige Gäste*, by contrast, is a psychologically sensitive social novel, perhaps the work of Raabe that most closely resembles the mode of Theodor Fontane.

Zum wilden Mann looks like another of Raabe's assaults on his public, insofar as it violates expectations of poetic justice more crassly than any other work; his contemporaries seem to have been more frightened than offended by it (see Sammons 1987, 231-32). The critical problem has therefore been to assess the meaning of Agonista's apparently radical evil, if it has any, as well as the character of his victim Kristeller. In the existentialist atmosphere after World War II Roloff saw Agonista's evil effect as unintentional and accidental; the story rather shows the fragility of the easily destroyed idyll. He links the novella's tragic pessimism not to Schopenhauer but to a European mood after mid-century, visible in Flaubert, Daudet, the Goncourts, Zola, Turgenyev, and the Scandinavians (Roloff [Sen.] 1949b, 45-47, 32-33). A commentator working from the Critical Theory of the Frankfurt School sees Agonista as a figuration of Darwinist ruthlessness under the entrepreneurial capitalism of the *Gründerzeit*; Kristeller is also a capitalist but is not daring enough, as he is blinded in his alienation. Raabe may have been sympathetic to Kristeller, but he did not understand his own character (Thürmer 1976, 153-53, 157-61). More recently, a rather speculative effort has been made to see the novella as a story of a pact with the devil and therefore a gloss on Goethe (Hoffmann 1986). As I have mentioned earlier (above, pp. 96-97), this argument has been continued by Heinrich Detering.

The traditional view of Kristeller has been to regard him, like Velten Andres, as a victor on the ideal plane in his truth to himself (e.g., Spruth 1955). Even Katherine Starr Kaiser, who describes the confrontation of Agonista and Kristeller as a contrast between a cosmopolitan adventurer and a provincial philistine, concludes that Kristeller is a victor (Kaiser 1974, 37-39). Of the older critics, only the Jesuit Perquin, to my knowledge, cast doubt on this interpretation, seeing a moral defect in Kristeller's lack of insight into injustice (Perquin 1927, 182-84). I tried to make the case that Kristeller's inner victory destroys the peace and comfort of his sister and that therefore Raabe does not consider him flawless (Sammons 1987, 232-34). I also argue that the text offers a clear explanation for Agonista's evil, namely through blood inheritance from his executioner forebears (236-37). I suspect critics have shied away from this because of its connection with nineteenth-century race theory; however, it was an interest of Raabe's that will bear some impartial scrutiny.

In regard to *Unruhige Gäste* there have been two related foci of interest: the novel's extraordinary texture of biblical allusiveness and the estimation of Phöbe's character. In the past the work seemed to be a gift to those clergymen and their allies determined to rescue a religious dimension to Raabe despite his undeniable institutional and doctrinal indifference. Pongs continued this tradition by seeing the whole constellation of the novel as religiously permeated (Pongs 1958, 499), and as late as 1966 a strongly Christianized interpretation was able to appear (Gruenter 1966), even though three years before the East German liberal Joachim Müller had observed that "wo Raabe in den religiösen Grund lotet, stößt er auch auf den Sand des Zweifels" (Müller 1963, 102). In that same year of 1966, a remarkable dissertation was completed at Mannheim by the literary scholar and, latterly, Christian Democratic politician Gertrud Höhler; it appeared in book form in 1969. Höhler's exposure and analysis of the virtually obsessive biblical intertextuality of the novel is the most illuminating study of Raabe's allusiveness since the work of Herman Meyer. She tends to see the story as deterministic and pessimistic, and makes a number of acute observations, for example, that Veit von Bielow wants to make the sources of Phöbe's security useful to himself (Höhler 1969, 93, 106). Though Höhler is aware that Raabe has been misinterpreted by religious partisans and claims no interest in his own religiosity (3-4), at the end she seems to fall somewhat into an existentialist-theological diction; at times it seems that she looks at the story through the orthodox lens of Prudens Hahnemeyer, even though she is aware of his unshriven state. Of Phöbe, Höhler interestingly remarks that she belongs to a type peculiar to German literature, exemplified by Ottilie in Goethe's *Wahlverwandtschaften*, Thekla in Schiller's *Wallenstein*, Natalie in Stifter's *Nachsommer*, and Anna in Keller's *Der grüne Heinrich* (126), adding that she is a sisterly figure not imaginable as an erotic partner (131), a point on which I strongly disagree.

In the past Phöbe was regarded as a saint, the paragon of all of Raabe's female figures. Pongs speculated as to whether she might have been modelled on Florence Nightingale (Pongs 1958, 511). Recently there has been a tendency to take a more negative view of Phöbe. Schedlinsky, whose economic and class-based interpretation has a number of good observations, though his insistence on repressive, authoritarian Christianity as a superstructural device of exploitation is quite alien to the text, rather oddly must take the part of Veit, about whose class status and limitations he is quite clear, against Phöbe. He sees her failing Veit's purpose of liberating her and helping her to overcome her infantile faith (Schedlinsky 1980, 353-56, 362, 373, 375-76). Also English-language criticism has taken up versions of this view. Webster claimed that Phöbe

> retreats behind a wall of faith and personal piety when the sensual instincts unconsciously aroused by Veit and made painfully explicit by Valerie threaten to interfere with the serene tenor of the life she had been leading up to that point. (Webster 1979b, 234-35).

Opie had earlier seen Phöbe as a naive child "with no real understanding of the mental struggles of the adult characters around her," arguing that she has done positive harm to Veit and has unwittingly precipitated a tragedy (Opie 1971, 175, 176-78, 179).

This is one matter on which I disagree with a tendency of modern criticism. I take Phöbe to be a wholly positive figure, a clever woman of natural erotic potentiality, latently capable of emancipation from the primitive religiosity that has repressed and deflected her (and from her brother Prudens, who wields it as an instrument of domination), but victimized by Veit's inattentiveness to the meaning of his own actions and thrust back into her repressed state (Sammons 1987, 244-47). However that may be, the record of criticism on these two works is a good example of the way Raabe's texts can continue to challenge and engage interpretation, and in their vitality, multiperspectivism, and shrewdness resist closure.

7: Epilogue:
Some Lessons on Reception History

HERMANN HELMERS WROTE IN THE PREFACE to his Sammlung
Metzler volume:

> Der Raabe des Jahres 1968 ist ein unsentimentaler
> Rationalist, ein zweifelnder Spötter, ein mutiger Streiter, ein
> humanitärer Politiker, ein wahrhaftiger Poet, ein scharfer
> Kritiker. Haben *wir* uns geändert? Hat *Raabe* sich geändert?
> Es besteht aller Grund zur Annahme, daß die ältere Raabe-
> Forschung die in die Zukunft weisenden Tendenzen des
> Werkes gar nicht oder falsch verstanden hat. (Helmers
> 1968b, v)

Some such confidence is detectable throughout the corpus of
contemporary Raabe criticism, and underlies much of its *élan* and
its sense of discovery. The critical tradition of the past can in good
conscience be repudiated. Raabe has appeared to our generation as a
new topic. Sometimes one could almost imagine that he were a
new writer of our own time just come upon the horizon and
welcomed enthusiastically by the critics. A symptom of this is the
continuing stress on his "modernity," in clear opposition to the
conservative, static, or retrograde character that had previously
been imposed upon him.

At the same time this critical self-confidence stands in
contradiction to a significant strand of literary theory that
developed contemporaneously with it: the parallel though not
entirely congruent doctrines of reception hermeneutics and
reception history. Strictly speaking, these doctrines are grounded in
an epistemological principle that the literary work exists in the
consciousness of the reader, not in the text and certainly not in the
intentionality of the author. They have been part of an effort to
reject the privileged authority of professional (in practice, usually
academic) critics and restore that of the reader as creative subject.
There would be much to say about this trend and the problems it

brings with it (see Sammons 1977, 104-05; Holub 1984). Here I just wish to point out how the peculiarities of the Raabe case highlight the more general difficulty.

It has seemed to me that theory and practice of reception history have been rather divergent. The theory would seem to have a relativizing force; it implies that all reception is adequate to its object in its own way. There is no firm meaning to be discovered in the text, since meaning is imposed by the reader; it changes from reader to reader and particularly diachronically, as a function of changing ideologically and historically formed consciousness. By deprivileging the established criticism of tradition it appears to deprivilege our own as well. But, perhaps not altogether astonishingly, this is not quite what has happened. For most systematic reception history has been a chronicle of misreadings. It does not take a certified logician to observe that the concept of misreading implies a possibility of right reading, and, on the whole, the right readings have turned out to be our own. One reason for this is that reception history has been a part of the more general tendency to arraign the bourgeois culture of the past. This affect is doubtless detectable in the modern criticism of all Western literatures — it is evidently one of the motives of deconstruction, especially in its Marxoid-Freudian and feminist variants — but it is particularly intense in German literary scholarship owing to its terrible historical burdens. If, however, reception history is employed in this way, the principle that the reader is the creator of the text is seriously compromised if not, in fact, silently jettisoned.

Without wishing to prejudice the theoretical question, I would suggest that the empirical record of modern Raabe criticism implies the following principles:

1. The apprehension of Raabe in the past, growing out of a tradition of those who knew him personally, in its main lines misperceived him ideologically and aesthetically, and came to misplace him altogether as it was assimilated into a fascist *Weltanschauung*. Not to put too fine a point on it, the Raabe criticism of the past is, by and large, *wrong*.

2. We, on the other hand, have learned to apprehend him, if not correctly, at least more adequately. We are *less wrong*; a lot less wrong, I expect, in the minds of most of us, including myself.

3. Much of this has been accomplished, not directly by an

ideological reversal (though that may be one of its underlying motives), but by the application of modern methods of literary criticism to a corpus that had been previously treated as a scripture available less to criticism than to exegesis. By the simple expedient of attending first, not to what the text says, but to how it is made, a whole world of irony, subtlety, critique, artistic dexterity, and polyperspectivism has been opened up. This, by the way, is not a trick. It would not be workable, for example, on Wilhelm Jensen.

4. Insofar as we have been doing what Raabe quite insistently wanted us to do, namely to read the texts themselves attentively with an effort in some way proportional to the effort of creation that went into them, we may be entitled to feel that we are more faithful to the author's "intention" than the commentators of the past.

5. The less professional the criticism, the less we like it. This is a touchy point that needs to be faced. In much modern critical theory there is a streak of wistful, utopian populism. It is strongest in Marxism, with its longings for a lost paradise of an unalienated relationship of life and art, but it is detectable elsewhere, including some versions of reception theories. Raabe's case is unusual, not so much in that he had a wide readership — this is, of course, the case with many writers — but in that the popular reception is recoverable because it is so articulate. Thus one of the weak areas of reception theories, that most reception is silent and therefore unrecoverable, leaving us with the written record of professional criticism and literary echoes, is somewhat obviated in this case. But the circumstance in no way enriches our apprehension of the œuvre. The more populist the reception, the more we oppose it. Now of course we might say that this is a case subject to very particular historical determinants; someone might still be found who would wish to explain the distortive reception by the fact that the readership belonged to the detested bourgeoisie rather than the heroic, progressive proletariat, but it would not be easy to adduce a persuasive counterexample. What the practice so far seems to demonstrate instead is a belief that systematic, methodologically alert, historically and aesthetically trained criticism will yield the best understanding; that means, in most cases, professional, scholarly criticism.

Personally, I agree that this is so. To the objection that this is merely another expression of subjective interest, I would say only:

look at the results, and see. Evidence of this kind has brought me to the view that some of the epistemological foundations of reception theory, at least as a practical matter, are unsound. It does appear that there are better and worse ways to apprehend a literary text, concretizations that are more or less faithful to it as an object, that we can learn how to read more adequately and have learned something about it in this century, and that criticism can progress. Nevertheless, the skepticism toward the operations of one's own consciousness that reception theory is designed to provoke may still be usefully applied. That the criticism of the past seems *so* bad to us ought perhaps to make us cautious and even modest about our own claims.

In retrospect it appears to me that there has been a tendency to shape Raabe to our own preferences and values, perhaps not as violently as in the past, but nevertheless to a degree that may become more obvious in the future. Much of the discourse has an unmistakable, in the circumstances probably unavoidable, apologetic note. We have been propagating Raabe at the same time as we have been trying to understand him. The effect shows itself most clearly in the claims made of his "modernity," as though the modern were a canon of value. This is one attitude that does not seem congruent with his own self-understanding; he did not regard himself as a writer of the future as, for example, Heine did; publishing nothing after 1899, he clearly felt that he was not meant to be a twentieth-century writer (e. g., E 4: 167, 223). We have tended, it seems to me, to lift him somewhat out of the international Victorian age, though it was a great age of the novel and it is sufficient honor to have distinguished oneself in it. In our desire to rescue him from the baneful political embrace of his "friends," we have pulled him farther leftward than he would have liked or acknowledged. Helmers's influential denomination of him as a "Linksintellektueller" (1968b, 13), cannot, I think, be sustained. We have treated the problem of his relationship to the Jews — and more generally, to race theory, to Darwinism, and to other trends of his time — gingerly if not defensively. In our effort to appreciate his artistry we have opposed the apostolic view of him as a source of wisdom and *Lebenshilfe*, though he said often enough that it was his purpose to give solace to the burdened and the defeated. Perhaps it would be fair to say that of late we have not wanted to think very much about what it was in Raabe that nourished the cult that flourished in his wake. So much inclined have we been to see ourselves as superior to it that we have acted as though it were an ideological mystification that had nothing to do with Raabe himself. As a rule, however, reception history suggests strongly the unlikelihood that the criticism of the past is all wrong and that of the present all right.

The modern criticism of Raabe is, I believe, a triumphant achievement. It brings honor to the craft of literary criticism and scholarship. But it is far from a closed chapter, and significant, new, and different perspectives, ideas, and modes of understanding are inevitable.

Bibliography

WILHELM RAABE'S WORKS

1856. *Die Chronik der Sperlingsgasse*. Berlin: Stage.

1857a. *Ein Frühling*. Braunschweig: Vieweg.

1857b. "Der Weg zum Lachen." *Der Bazar* 3.

1857c. "Der Student von Wittenberg." *Westermann's Illustrirte Deutsche Monatshefte* 3 (14): 117-30.

1858a. "Weihnachtsgeister." *Hausblätter* 1: 321-39.

1858b. "Lorenz Scheibenhart. Ein Lebensbild aus wüster Zeit." *Westermann's Illustrirte Deutsche Monatshefte* 4 (20): 115-27.

1858c. "Einer aus der Menge." *Hausblätter* 4: 50-59.

1858d. "Die alte Universität." *Westermann's Illustrirte Deutsche Monatshefte* 5 (25): 1-11.

1858/59. "Der Junker von Denow." *Westermann's Illustrirte Deutsche Monatshefte* 5 (30): 583-602.

1859a. *Die Kinder von Finkenrode*. Berlin: Schotte.

1859b. *Halb Mähr, halb mehr! Erzählungen, Skizzen und Reime*. Berlin: Schotte. Comprises "Der Weg zum Lachen," "Der Student von Wittenberg," "Weihnachtsgeister," "Lorenz Scheibenhart," "Einer aus der Menge."

1859/60. "Wer kann es wenden?" *Westermann's Illustrirte Deutsche Monatshefte* 7 (39): 233-52.

1860a. "Aus dem Lebensbuch des Schulmeisterleins Michel Haas." *Westermann's Illustrirte Deutsche Monatshefte* 8 (44): 213-29.

1860b. "Ein Geheimniß. Lebensbild aus den Tagen Ludwigs XIV." *Westermanns Illustrirte Deutsche Monatshefte* 8 (48): 575-87.

1860/61. "Die schwarze Galeere." *Westermann's Illustrirte Deutsche Monatshefte* 9 (53): 465-88.

1861a. *Der heilige Born. Blätter aus dem Bilderbuch des sechzehnten Jahrhunderts.* Vienna and Prague: Kober & Markgraf.

1861b. *Nach dem großen Kriege. Eine Geschichte in zwölf Briefen.* Berlin: Schotte.

1861c. "Auf dunklem Grunde." *Westermann's Illustrirte Deutsche Monatshefte* 10 (58): 341-55.

1862a. *Unseres Herrgotts Canzlei.* Braunschweig: Westermann.

1862b. "Das letzte Recht." *Westermann's Illustrirte Deutsche Monatshefte* 12 (70): 407-30.

1863a. *Verworrenes Leben. Novellen und Skizzen.* Glogau: Flemming. Comprises "Die alte Universität," "Der Junker von Denow," "Aus dem Lebensbuch des Schulmeisterleins Michel Haas," "Wer kann es wenden?" "Ein Geheimnis."

1863b. *Die Leute aus dem Walde.* Braunschweig: Westermann.

1863c. "Eine Grabrede aus dem Jahre 1609." *Die Maje* 6 (1): 20-30.

1863d. "Hollunderblüthe. Eine Erinnerung aus dem 'Haus des Lebens.'" *Ueber Land und Meer* 10 (27): 417-19; (28): 433-35; (29): 449-51.

1863e. "Die Hämelschen Kinder." *Die Maje* 6 (6): 257-73.

1864. *Der Hungerpastor.* Berlin: Janke.

1864/65. "Keltische Knochen. Eine rührend-heitere Geschichte." *Westermann's Illustrirte Deutsche Monatshefte* N. S. 1 (97): 1-20.

1865a. *Drei Federn.* Berlin: Janke.

1865b. *Ferne Stimmen. Erzählungen.* Berlin: Janke. Comprises "Die schwarze Galeere," "Eine Grabrede aus dem Jahre 1609," "Das letzte Recht," "Hollunderblüthe."

1865c. "Else von der Tanne oder Das Glück Domini Friedemann Leutenbachers, armen Dieners am Wort Gottes zu Wallrode im Elend." *Freya* 5 (1): 1-7; (2): 46-55.

1866a. "Die Gänse von Bützow. Eine obotritische Historia." *Über Land und Meer* 15 (17): 257-59; (18): 274-75; (19): 289-91; (20): 305-07; (21): 322-23; (22): 338-39.

1866b. "Sankt Thomas." *Freya* 6: 233-40, 273-86.

1866c. "Gedelöcke. Eine absonderliche, doch wahre Geschichte." *Westermann's Illustrirte Deutsche Monatshefte* N. S. 4 (21): 297-317.

1866d. "Im Siegeskranze." *Ueber Land und Meer* 17 (3): 33-35; (4): 49-51; (5): 65-67.

1867. *Abu Telfan oder die Heimkehr vom Mondgebirge.* Stuttgart: Hallberger.

1868a. *Der Regenbogen. Sieben Erzählungen.* Stuttgart: Hallberger. Comprises volume 1, "Die Hämelschen Kinder," "Else von der Tanne," "Keltische Knochen," "Sankt Thomas"; volume 2, "Die Gänse von Bützow," "Gedelöcke," "Im Siegeskranze."

1868b. "Thekla's Erbschaft oder die Geschichte eines schwülen Tages." *Über Land und Meer* 21 (8): 113-16.

1870a. *Der Schüdderump.* Braunschweig: Westermann.

1870b. "Der Marsch nach Hause. Eine Soldatengeschichte aus alter Zeit." *Daheim* 6 (48): 754-56; (49): 770-74; (50): 786-90; (51): 802-05; (52): 818-20.

1870c. "Des Reiches Krone." *Ueber Land und Meer* 25 (1): 2-3; (2): 1-3; (3)): 1-3; (4): 14-15.

1872. *Der Dräumling.* Berlin: Janke.

1873a. *Deutscher Mondschein. Vier Erzählungen.* Stuttgart: Hallberger. Comprises "Deutscher Mondschein," "Der Marsch nach Hause," "Des Reiches Krone," "Thekla's Erbschaft."

1873b. *Christoph Pechlin. Eine internationale Liebesgeschichte.* Leipzig: Günther.

1874a. *Meister Autor oder die Geschichten vom versunkenen Garten*. Leipzig: Günther.

1874b. "Zum wilden Mann." *Westermann's Illustrirte Deutsche Monatshefte* 3rd S. 4 (19): 1-45.

1874/75a. "Eulenpfingsten." *Westermann's Illustrirte Deutsche Monatshefte* 3rd S. 5 (25: 1-21; (26): 113-36.

1874/75b. "Frau Salome." *Westermann's Illustrirte Deutsche Monatshefte* 3rd S. 5 (29): 449-94.

1875. "Höxter und Corvey." *Westermann's Illustrirte Deutsche Monatshefte* 3rd S. 6 (31): 1-16; (32): 113-42.

1875/76. "Vom alten Proteus. Eine Hochsommergeschichte." *Westermann's Illustrirte Deutsche Monatshefte* 3rd S. 7 (39): 225-68.

1876a. *Horacker*. Berlin: Grote.

1876b. "Die Innerste." *Westermann's Illustrirte Deutsche Monatshefte* 3rd S. 8 (46): 337-57; (47): 449-73.

1878. "Auf dem Altenteil. Eine Sylvesterstimmung und Neujahrsgeschichte." *Deutsches Montagsblatt* (52).

1879a. *Krähenfelder Geschichten*. Braunschweig: Westermann. Comprises volume 1, "Zum wilden Mann," "Höxter und Corvey"; volume 2, "Eulenpfingsten"; volume 3, "Frau Salome," "Die Innerste," "Vom alten Proteus."

1879b. *Wunnigel*. Braunschweig: Westermann.

1880a. *Alte Nester. Zwei Bücher Lebensgeschichten*. Braunschweig: Westermann.

1880b. *Deutscher Adel*. Braunschweig: Westermann.

1881. *Das Horn von Wanza*. Braunschweig: Westermann.

1882. *Fabian und Sebastian*. Braunschweig: Westermann.

1883. *Prinzessin Fisch*. Braunschweig: Westermann.

1884a. *Pfisters Mühle. Ein Sommerferienheft*. Leipzig: Grunow.

1884b. *Villa Schönow*. Braunschweig: Westermann.

1884c. "Ein Besuch." *Illustrirte Zeitung* 83 (2152): 316-17.

1886. *Unruhige Gäste. Ein Roman aus dem Saekulum*. Berlin: Grote.

1887. *Im alten Eisen*. Berlin: Grote.

1889a. *Der Lar. Eine Oster-, Pfingst-, Weihnachts- und Neujahrsgeschichte*. Braunschweig: Westermann.

1889b. *Das Odfeld*. Leipzig: Elischer.

1891. *Stopfkuchen. Eine See- und Mordgeschichte*. Berlin: Janke.

1892. *Gutmanns Reisen*. Berlin: Janke.

1894. *Kloster Lugau*. Berlin: Janke.

1896. *Die Akten des Vogelsangs*. Berlin: Janke.

1896-1900. *Gesammelte Erzählungen*. Berlin: Janke. 4 volumes.

1899. *Hastenbeck*. Berlin: Janke.

1911. *Altershausen*. Berlin: Janke.

1912. "Der gute Tag." *Daheim* 48 (17): 19-24; (18): 18-24.

1913-16. *Sämtliche Werke*. 18 volumes in three series. Berlin-Grunewald: Klemm.

1934. *Sämtliche Werke*. 15 volumes in three series. Berlin-Grunewald: Klemm.

1960- . *Sämtliche Werke*, ed. Karl Hoppe et al. 20 volumes plus supplementary volumes. Göttingen: Vandenhoeck & Ruprecht (begun 1951. Braunschweig: Klemm).

WORKS CITED IN CHRONOLOGICAL ORDER

The following abbreviations are used throughout:

Mitt. = *Mitteilungen für die Gesellschaft der Freunde Wilhelm Raabes* (1911-43): *Der Raabefreund* (1944); *Mitteilungen der Raabe-Gesellschaft* (1948-).

RJ = *Jahrbuch der Raabe-Gesellschaft* (1960-). The *RJ* lacks volume numbers.

Morsier, Edouard de. 1890. "Wilhelm Raabe." Morsier, *Romanciers allemands contemporains*. Paris: Perrin et Cie. 313-401.

Gerber, Paul. 1897. *Wilhelm Raabe: Eine Würdigung seiner Dichtungen*. Leipzig: Wilhelm Friedrich.

Berg, Leo. 1901. "Wilhelm Raabe als Erzähler (1897)"; "Hastenbeck." Berg, *Neue Essays*. Oldenburg and Leipzig: Schulze. 269-83, 426-33.

_____. 1905. "Wilhelm Raabe." Berg, *Aus der Zeit — Gegen die Zeit. Gesammelte Essays*. Berlin: Hüpeden & Merzyn. 51-66.

Brandes, Wilhelm. 1906. *Wilhelm Raabe: Sieben Kapitel zum Verständnis und zur Würdigung des Dichters*. 2nd ed. Wolfenbüttel and Berlin: Julius Zwissler, Otto Janke.

Doernenburg, Emil. 1908. See Doernenburg and Fehse 1921.

Speyer, Marie. 1908. *Raabes "Hollunderblüte."* Regensburg: Habbel.

Bass, Josef. 1910. "Die Juden bei Wilhelm Raabe." *Monatsschrift für Geschichte und Wissenschaft der Juden* 54: 641-88.

Junge, Hermann. 1910. *Wilhelm Raabe: Studien über Form und Inhalt seiner Werke*. Dortmund: Ruhfus.

Mehring, Franz. 1910. "Wilhelm Raabe. Dezember 1910." Mehring 1961. *Aufsätze zur deutschen Literatur von Hebbel bis Schweichel. Gesammelte Schriften*, ed. Thomas Höhle et al. Vol. 11: Berlin: Dietz. 97-99.

Elster, Otto, and Hanns Martin Elster, eds. 1911. *Wilhelm Raabe-Kalender auf das Jahr 1912*. Berlin: Grote.

Krüger, Herm. Anders. 1911. *Der junge Raabe: Jugendjahre und Erstlingswerke. Nebst einer Bibliographie der Werke Raabes und der Raabeliteratur*. Leipzig: Xenien-Verlag.

Elster, Otto, and Hanns Martin Elster, eds. 1912. *Wilhelm Raabe-Kalender*. Berlin: Grote.
Includes:
Bass, Josef. 1912. "Wie ich zu Wilhelm Raabe kam. Mit vier Briefen des Dichters." 129-35.
Junge, Hermann. 1912a. "Wilhelm Raabe und das Christentum." 162-68.

Goebel, Heinrich, ed. 1912. *Raabe-Gedächtnisschrift*. Leipzig: Xenien-Verlag.
Includes:
Junge, Hermann. 1912b. "Raabes Pastorengestalten." 139-49.

Meyer, Richard M. 1912. *Die deutsche Literatur des Neunzehnten Jahrhunderts*. Berlin: Bondi.

Doernenburg, Emil. 1913. "Wilhelm Raabe in Amerika." *Mitt.* 3: 97-109. Reprinted Bauer 1925, 72-83.

Elster, Otto, and Hanns Martin Elster, eds. 1913. *Wilhelm Raabe-Kalender 1914*. Berlin: Grote.

Schiller, Herbert. 1917. *Die innere Form W. Raabes*. Borna-Leipzig: Noske.

Bönneken, Margarete. 1918. See Bönneken 1926.

Doernenburg, Emil. 1919. *Wilhelm Raabe und die deutsche Romantik*. Philadelphia: Americana Germanica Press.

Bauer, Constantin, and Hans Martin Schultz, eds. 1921. *Raabe-Gedenkbuch: Im Auftrage der Gesellschaft der Freunde Wilhelm Raabes. Zum 90. Geburtstag des Dichters*. Berlin-Grunewald: Klemm.

Doernenburg, Emil, and Wilhelm Fehse. 1921. *Raabe und Dickens: Ein Beitrag zur Erkenntnis der geistigen Gestalt Wilhelm Raabes*. Magdeburg: Creutz.

Fehse, Wilhelm. 1921. "Die literarischen Symbole in den 'Akten des Vogelsangs.' Ein Nachruf auf Dr. Margarete Bönneken." *Mitt.* 11: 8-20, 33-57.

Stockum, Th. C. van. 1921. "Schopenhauer und Raabe, Pessimismus und Humor." *Neophilologus* 6: 169-84.

Fehse, Wilhelm. 1922. "Goethe, Raabe und die deutsche Zukunft." *Mitt.* 12: 11-25.

_____. 1924. "Raabes Erzählung 'Frau Salome.' Ihre Entstehung und ihre Deutungen." *Mitt.* 14: 41-58.

Jensch, Fritz. 1924. "Unaufgeklärte Zitate bei Raabe." *Mitt.* 14: 140-47.

Silz, Walter. 1924a "Freytag's *Soll und Haben* and Raabe's *Der Hungerpastor*." *Modern Language Notes* 39: 10-18.

_____. 1924b. "Pessimism in Raabe's Stuttgart Trilogy." *Publications of the Modern Language Association* 39: 687-704.

Spiero, Heinrich. 1924. See Spiero [1925].

Bauer, Constantin, ed. 1925. *Raabestudien: Im Auftrag der "Gesellschaft der Freunde Wilhelm Raabes."* Wolfenbüttel: Heckner.

Dose, Helene. 1925. *Aus Wilhelm Raabes mystischer Werkstatt.* Hamburg: Hanseatische Verlagsanstalt.

Jensch, Fritz. 1925. *Wilhelm Raabes Zitatenschatz.* Wolfenbüttel: Heckner.

Spiero, Heinrich. [1925]. *Raabe: Leben — Werk — Wirkung.* Wittenberg: Ziemsen.

Ahrbeck, Hans. 1926. *Wilhelm Raabes Stopfkuchen: Studien zu Gehalt und Form von Raabes Erzählungen.* Borna-Leipzig: Noske.

Bönneken, Margarete. 1926. *Wilhelm Raabes Roman "Die Akten des Vogelsangs."* 2nd ed. Marburg: Elwert.

Heess, Wilhelm. [1926]. *Raabe: Seine Zeit und seine Berufung.* Berlin-Grunewald: Klemm.

Jensch, Fritz. 1926. "Unaufgeklärte Zitate bei Raabe. Nachträge." *Mitt.* 16: 204-07.

Mohr, Heinrich. 1927. "Wilhelm Raabe und die nordische Rasse." *Mitt.* 17: 18-39.

Perquin, Nicolaas Cornelis Adrianus S. J. 1927. *Wilhelm Raabes Motive als Ausdruck seiner Weltanschauung.* Amsterdam: H. J. Paris.

Spiero, Heinrich. [1927]. *Raabe-Lexikon.* Berlin-Grunewald: Klemm.

Zornemann, Erich B. 1927. "Herbert Schillers Angriff auf Raabes Künstlertum. Ein Versuch zur Klärung." *Mitt.* 17: 129-38.

Dose, Helene. 1928. *Die Magie bei Wilhelm Raabe.* Berlin-Grunewald: Klemm.

Fehse, Wilhelm. 1928. *Wilhelm Raabes Leben.* Berlin-Grunewald: Klemm.

Jensch, Fritz. 1928. "Unaufgeklärte Zitate bei Raabe. Nachträge." *Mitt.* 18: 39-41.

_____. 1929. "Unaufgeklärte Zitate bei Raabe. Nachträge." *Mitt.* 19: 87-92.

Röttger, Friedrich. 1930. *Volk und Vaterland bei Wilhelm Raabe.* Graz: Stiasny.

Brües, Otto. 1931. "Raabe und die junge Generation." *Mitt.* 21: 47-55.

Goebel, Heinrich. 1931. *Raabe-Gedächtnisschrift.* New, revised ed. Hildesheim and Leipzig: Lax.
Includes:
Bass, Josef. 1931. "Die jüdischen Gestalten bei Raabe." 62-90.

Hertel, Heinz. 1931. "Wie stellt sich die heutige Jugend zu Raabe?" *Mitt.* 21: 59-61.

Jensch, Fritz. 1931. "Unaufgeklärte Zitate bei Raabe. Nachträge." *Mitt.* 21: 71-75.

Kientz, Louis. 1931. "Raabe und Frankreich." *Mitt.* 21: 130-36.

Schultz, Hans Martin. 1931. *Raabe-Schriften: Eine systematische Darstellung.* Wolfenbüttel: Heckner.

Spiero, Heinrich, ed. 1931. *Wilhelm Raabe und sein Lebenskreis: Festschrift zum 100. Geburtstag des Dichters namens der Gesellschaft der Freunde Wilhelm Raabes und der Verlagsanstalt Hermann Klemm A. G.* Berlin-Grunewald: Klemm.
Includes:
Junge, Hermann. 1931. "Raabes religiöse Lebensdeutung." 21-24.

Westerburg, Hans. 1931. "Wilhelm Raabe als Ethiker." *Mitt.* 21: 145-56.

Guardini, Romano. 1932. See Helmers 1968a.

Naumann, Hans. 1932. "Braunschweiger Festrede über Wilh. Raabe." *Mitt.* 22: 1-13.

Hahne, Franz. 1933a. "Raabe und die nationale Revolution." *Mitt.* 23: 67-69.

_____. 1933b. "Raabes Stellung im dritten Reich." *Mitt.* 23: 97-110.

Martini, Fritz. 1933a. "Wilhelm Raabe und das literarische Biedermeier." *Mitt.* 23: 33-45.

_____. 1933b. "Wilhelm Raabe und das XIX. Jahrhundert." *Zeitschrift für deutsche Philologie* 58: 326-43.

Pongs, Hermann. 1933. "Raabe und das Reich." *Mitt.* 23: 1-13.

Fehse, Wilhelm. 1934. "Dämon und Tyche." *Mitt.* 24: 101-14.

Hahne, Franz. 1934. "Raabe vom Rassenstandpunkt betrachtet." *Mitt.* 24: 114-22.

Iltz, Johannes. 1934. "Raabe und Hitler." *Mitt.* 24: 8-17.

Martini, Fritz. 1934a. "Der Bauer in der Dichtung Wilhelm Raabes." *Mitt.* 24: 69-77.

_____. 1934b. *Die Stadt in der Dichtung Wilhelm Raabes.* Greifswald: Hans Alder, E. Parzig & Co.

_____. 1935. "Das Problem des Realismus im 19. Jahrhundert und die Dichtung Wilhelm Raabes." *Dichtung und Volkstum* 36: 271-302.

Hartmann, Fritz. 1936. "Im Silberkranz. Unser erstes Vierteljahrhundert." *Mitt.* 26: 123-34.

Schneider, Hilde, 1936. *Wilhelm Raabes Mittel der epischen Darstellung.* Berlin: Ebering.

Coenen, F. E. 1937. "Wilhelm Raabe's Treatment of the Emigrant." *Studies in Philology* 34: 612-26.

Fehse, Wilhelm. 1937. *Wilhelm Raabe: Sein Leben und seine Werke.* Braunschweig: Vieweg.

Junge, Hermann. 1938. "Wilhelm Raabes Religiosität." *Mitt.* 28: 20-21.

Weinhardt, Reinhold. 1938. "Schopenhauer in Wilhelm Raabes Werken." *Jahrbuch der Schopenhauer-Gesellschaft* 25: 306-28.

Hahne, Franz. 1939. "Raabes Sehnen und des Führers Erfüllung." *Mitt.* 29: 33-35.

Kientz, Louis. 1939. *Wilhelm Raabe: L'homme, la pensée et l'œuvre.* Paris: Didier.

Fehse, Wilhelm. 1940a. " *In alls gedultig.*" *Briefe Wilhelm Raabes (1842-1910).* Berlin: Grote.

_____. 1940b. *Raabe und Jensen: Denkmal einer Lebensfreundschaft.* Berlin: Grote.

Lukács, Georg. 1940. See Lukács 1952.

Meinerts, Hans Jürgen. 1940. *"Die Akten des Vogelsangs": Raabestudien auf Grund einer Sprachuntersuchung.* Berlin: Junker und Dünnhaupt.

Albaugh, Kathryn Louise. 1941. "The Influence of William Makepeace Thackeray on Wilhelm Raabe." Diss. Stanford University.

Vogelsang, Günther. 1942. *Das Ich als Schicksal und Aufgabe in den Dichtungen Raabes.* Braunschweig: Appelhans.

Meyer, Herman. 1943. See Meyer 1963.

Pongs, Hermann. 1944. "Frauenehre bei Raabe." *Mitt.* 34 (2): 3-18.

Roloff, Ernst-August [Senior], ed. 1946. *Wilhelm Raabe Kalender 1947.* Goslar: Deutsche Volksbücherei.
Includes:
Fuchtel, Paul. 1946. "Die Wilhelm-Raabe-Gesellschaft." 145-48.
Spiero, Heinrich. 1946. "Wilhelm Raabe und Berlin." 47-50.

Roloff, Ernst August [Senior], ed. 1948. *Wilhelm Raabe Kalender 1948.* Goslar: Deutsche Volksbücherei.

Butzmann, Hans. 1949. "Musäus' Schatzgräber und Raabes Erzählung 'Zum wilden Mann.'" *Mitt.* 36: 81-83.

Heinrich, Thea. 1949. "Der Tod in der Dichtung Wilhelm Raabes." Diss. University of Munich.

Roloff, Ernst-August [Senior], ed. 1949a. *Raabe-Jahrbuch.* Braunschweig: Appelhans.

Includes:
Roloff, Ernst August [Senior]. 1949b. "Triumph und Überwin-
    dung der Kanaille. Raabes Pessimismus im Spiegel der
    Novelle 'Zum wilden Mann.'" 30-53.

Vogel, Maria. 1949. "Darstellung der von Wilhelm Raabe ge-
    schilderten seelischen Abnormalitäten und Versuch einer
    psychiatrischen Deutung." M. D. Diss. University of Frankfurt
    am Main.

Hajek, Siegfried. Der Mensch und die Welt im Werk Wilhelm
    Raabes. Warendorf: Verlag J. Schnellsche Buchhandlung (C.
    Leopold).

Roloff, Ernst-August [Senior], ed. 1950. Raabe-Jahrbuch. Braun-
    schweig: Appelhans.
Includes:
Hahne, Franz. 1950. "Raabe und der Harz." 109-17.

Schmitz, Christel. 1950. "Das Todesproblem im Werk Wilhelm
    Raabes." Diss. University of Bonn.

Bauer, Constantin. 1951. "Die Anfänge der Raabe-Gesellschaft."
    Mitt. 38 (2): 2-8.

Buchholz, Walter. 1951. "Ein Nachwort zu Wilhelm Raabes
    'Stopfkuchen.'" Mitt. 38 (1): 6-11.

Roloff, Ernst August [Junior]. 1951a. "Aus der Chronik der Raabe-
    Gesellschaft." Mitt. 38 (2): 8-14.

_____. 1951b. "Wilhelm Raabes Entwicklungsroman
    'Prinzessin Fisch' und seine Bedeutung für das Gesamtwerk."
    Diss. University of Göttingen.

Weniger, Erich. 1951. See Helmers 1968a.

Neumann, Friedrich. 1951/52. "Wilhelm Raabes Schüdderump."
    Zeitschrift für deutsche Philologie 71: 291-329.

Fairley, Barker. 1952. "The Modernity of Wilhelm Raabe." German
    Studies Presented to Leonard Ashley Willoughby by Pupils,
    Colleagues and Friends on his Retirement, [ed. J. Boyd]. Oxford:
    Blackwell. 66-81. Reprinted 1984 in Fairley, Selected Essays on
    German Literature, ed. Rodney Symington. New York, Berne,
    Frankfurt am Main, and Nancy: Peter Lang. 253-71.

Lukács, Georg. 1952. "Wilhelm Raabe." *Deutsche Realisten des 19. Jahrhunderts*. Berlin: Aufbau. 231-61. Reprinted Helmers 1968a, 44-73.

Esser, Aloise. 1953. "Zeitgestaltung und Struktur in den historischen Novellen Wilhelm Raabes." Diss. University of Bonn.

Heim, Karl. 1953. "Wilhelm Raabe und das Publikum." Diss. University of Tübingen.

Martini, Fritz. 1953. "Wilhelm Raabes 'Höxter und Corvey.'" *Der Deutschunterricht* 5 (1): 76-92.

Meyer, Herman. 1953. See Helmers 1968a.

Roloff, Ernst-August [Senior]. 1953. "Wilhelm Raabe in zeitgenössischer Kritik." *Mitt.* 40 (2): 12-20.

Pascal, Roy. 1954. "The Reminiscence-Technique in Raabe." *Modern Language Review* 49: 339-48. Republished as "Die Erinnerungstechnik bei Raabe." Helmers 1968a, 130-44.

Senk, Herbert. 1954. "Bemerkungen zu Raabes Federzeichnungen." *Mitt.* 41: 110-30.

Brill, E. V. K. 1954/55. "Raabe's Reception in England." *German Life & Letters* N. S. 8: 304-12.

Fairley, Barker. 1955. "Das Moderne an Wilhelm Raabe's Erzähltechnik." *Mitt.* 42: 74-89.

Heim, Karl. 1955. "Wilhelm Raabe und das Publikum." *Mitt.* 42: 1-12.

Senk, Herbert. 1955. "Zur Datierung und Komposition der Bleistiftzeichnung 'Der philiströse Sisyphus.'" *Mitt.* 42: 55-58.

Spruth, Paul. 1955. "Zur Psychologie des Apothekers Philipp Kristeller und des Obersten Don Agostin Agonista in Raabes Novelle 'Zum wilden Mann.'" *Mitt.* 42: 101-03.

Bauer, Constantin. 1956. "Raabe im Ausland." *Mitt.* 43: 1-10.

Fairley, Barker, ed. 1956. Wilhelm Raabe, *Pfisters Mühle. Ein Sommerferienheft*. London: Duckworth.

Pascal, Roy. 1956. *The German Novel*. Toronto: University of Toronto Press.

Senk, Herbert. 1956. "Der Kontrast als Ausdrucksmittel in Raabes Erzählungen und Zeichnungen." *Mitt.* 43: 59-65.

Butzmann, Hans. 1957. See Dittrich 1984.

Oppermann, Hans. 1957. "Wilhelm Fehse." *Mitt.* 44: 66-72.

Pongs, Hermann. 1958. *Wilhelm Raabe: Leben und Werk.* Heidelberg: Quelle & Meyer.

Weniger, Erich. 1958. "'Erlebnis' und 'Dichtung' in Werk Wilhelm Raabes." *Die Sammlung* 13: 613-23.

Martini, Fritz. 1959. See Helmers 1968a.

Hebbel, Christa. 1960. "Die Funktion der Erzähler- und Figurenperspektiven in Wihelm Raabes Ich-Erzählungen." Diss. University of Heidelberg.

Helmers, Hermann. 1960. *Die bildenden Mächte in den Romanen Wilhelm Raabes.* Weinheim: Beltz.

Hoppe, Karl. 1960a. "Aphorismen Raabes chronologisch geordnet." *RJ.* 94-139. Reprinted Hoppe 1967, 87-129.

_____. 1960b. *Wilhelm Raabe als Zeichner.* Göttingen: Vandenhoeck & Ruprecht.

Majut, Rudolf. 1960. "Der deutsche Roman vom Biedermeier bis zur Gegenwart." *Deutsche Philologie im Aufriß*, ed. Wolfgang Stammler et al. 2nd ed. Vol. 2. Berlin: Erich Schmidt Verlag. Cols. 1357-1535.

Mayer, Gerhart. 1960. *Die geistige Entwicklung Wilhelm Raabes: Dargestellt unter besonderer Berücksichtigung seines Verhältnisses zur Philosophie.* Göttingen: Vandenhoeck & Ruprecht.

Butler, Geoffrey Patrick Guyton. 1961. "England and America in the Writings of Wilhelm Raabe: A Critical Study of his Knowledge and Appreciation of Language, Literature and People." Diss. University of London.

Fairley, Barker. 1961. *Wilhelm Raabe: An Introduction to his Novels.* Oxford: Clarendon Press.

Hoppe, Karl. 1961. "Wilhelm Raabe einst und heute." *RJ*. 7-20. Reprinted Helmers 1968a, 173-84.

Maatje, Frank C. 1961a. "Ein früher Ansatz zur 'Stream of Consciousness'-Dichtung: Wilhelm Raabes 'Altershausen.'" *Neophilologus* 45: 305-23.

_____. 1961b. "Der Raum als konstituierendes Element in Wilhelm Raabes 'Hungerpastor.'" *Levende Talen* 211: 515-21. Reprinted Helmers 1968a, 185-91.

Meyer, Herman. 1961. "Wilhelm Raabe. 'Hastenbeck.'" Meyer, *Das Zitat in der Erzählkunst: Zur Geschichte und Poetik des europäischen Romans*. Stuttgart: Metzler. 186-206.

Oppermann, Hans. 1961. "Wilhelm Raabe der Dichter." *RJ*. 21-39.

Goetz, Marketa. 1962. "The Short Stories: A Possible Clue to Wilhelm Raabe." *Germanic Review* 37: 55-67.

Helmers, Hermann. 1962. "Über Wilhelm Raabes Sprache." *RJ*. 9-21.

Klein, Johannes. "Vorwegnahme moderner Formen in Raabes 'Gänsen von Bützow.'" *RJ*. 99-107. Reprinted Helmers 1968a, 192-99.

Mayer, Gerhart. 1962. "Raabes Romanfragment 'Altershausen' I. Teil." *RJ*. 155-65. Reprinted Helmers 1968a, 211-19.

Müller, Joachim. 1962. "Erzählstruktur und Symbolgefüge in Wilhelm Raabes 'Unruhigen Gästen.' I. Die Erzählstruktur." *RJ*. 121-35.

Pascal, Roy. 1962. "Warum ist 'Altershausen' Fragment geblieben?" *RJ*. 147-54.

Stammler, Heinrich. 1962. See Helmers 1968a.

Helmers, Hermann. 1963. "Die Verfremdung als epische Grundtendenz im Werk Raabes." *RJ*. 7-30.

Hoppe, Karl. 1963. "Aus Raabes Briefwechsel." *RJ*. 31-63. Reprinted Hoppe 1967, 39-76.

Killy, Walter. 1963. See Helmers 1968a.

Mayer, Gerhart. 1963. "Raabes Romanfragment 'Altershausen': Grundzüge einer Interpretation II. Teil." *RJ*. 64-75. Reprinted Helmers 1968a, 219-28.

Meyer, Herman. 1963. *Der Sonderling in der deutschen Literatur*. Munich: Hanser.

Müller, Joachim. 1963. "Erzählstruktur und Symbolgefüge in Wilhelm Raabes 'Unruhigen Gästen.' II. Das Symbolgefüge." *RJ*. 88-102.

Richter, Helmut, ed. [1963]. *Die Akte Wilhelm Raabe*. Weimar: Archiv der Deutschen Schillerstiftung.

Bramsted, E. K. 1964. *Aristocracy and the Middle-Classes in Germany: Social Types in German Literature 1830-1900*. Chicago and London: University of Chicago Press.

Maatje, Frank Christiaan. 1964. *Der Doppelroman: Eine literatursystematische Studie über duplikative Erzählstrukturen*. Groningen: Wolters.

Martini, Fritz. 1964. "Wilhelm Raabes 'Altershausen.'" *RJ*. 78-105.

Ohl, Hubert. 1964. See Helmers 1968a.

Oppermann, Hans. 1964. See Helmers 1968a.

Goldammer, Peter, and Helmut Richter, eds. 1964-66. Wilhelm Raabe, *Ausgewählte Werke in sechs Bänden*. Berlin und Weimar: Aufbau.

Fairley, Barker. 1966. "Nachwort." Wilhelm Raabe, *Die Chronik der Sperlingsgasse*. Frankfurt am Main and Berlin: Ullstein.

Gruenter, Rainer. 1966. "Ein *Schritt vom Wege*. Geistliche Lokalsymbolik in Wilhelm Raabes *Unruhige Gäste*." *Euphorion* 60: 209-21.

Hoppe, Else. 1966. "Wilhelm Raabe und Marie Jensen. Mythos einer Freundschaft." *RJ*. 25-57.

Oppermann, Hans. 1966. "Das Bild der Antike bei Wilhelm Raabe." *RJ*. 58-79.

Richter, Helmut. 1966. See Helmers 1968a.

Hoppe, Karl. 1967. *Wilhelm Raabe: Beiträge zum Verständnis seiner Person und seines Werkes*. Göttingen: Vandenhoeck & Ruprecht.

King, Janet K. 1967. "Raabe's *Else von der Tanne*." *German Quarterly* 40: 653-63.

Meyer, Herman. 1967. See Meyer 1968.

Hanson, William P. 1967/68. "Some Basic Themes in Raabe." *German Life & Letters* N. S. 21: 122-30.

Beaucamp, Eduard. 1968. *Literatur als Selbstdarstellung. Wilhelm Raabe und die Möglichkeiten eines deutschen Realismus*. Bonn: Bouvier.

Clyde, Monica Weber. 1968. "Der Bildungsgedanke bei Wilhelm Raabe." Diss. University of California, Berkeley.

Hellmann, Winfried. 1968. "Objektivität, Subjektivität und Erzählkunst. Zur Romantheorie Friedrich Spielhagens." *Deutsche Romantheorie: Beiträge zu einer historischen Poetik des Romans in Deutschland*, ed. Reinhold Grimm. Frankfurt am Main and Bonn: Athenäum. 165-217.

Helmers, Hermann, ed. 1968a. *Raabe in neuer Sicht*. Stuttgart, Berlin, Cologne, and Mainz: Kohlhammer.
Includes:
Guardini, Romano. 1932. "Über Wilhelm Raabes 'Stopfkuchen.'" 12-43.
Killy, Walter. 1963. "Geschichte gegen die Geschichte. 'Das Odfeld.'" 229-46.
Martini, Fritz. 1959. "Wilhelm Raabes 'Prinzessin Fisch.' Wirklichkeit und Dichtung im erzählenden Realismus des neunzehnten Jahrhunderts." 145-72.
Meyer, Herman. 1953. "Raum und Zeit in Wilhelm Raabes Erzählkunst." 98-129.
Ohl, Hubert. 1964. "Eduards Heimkehr oder Le Vaillant und das Riesenfaultier. Zu Wilhelm Raabes 'Stopfkuchen.'" 247-78.
Oppermann, Hans. 1964. "Zum Problem der Zeit bei Wilhelm Raabe." 294-311.
Richter, Helmut. 1966. "Die Chronik der Sperlingsgasse." 312-16.

Stammler, Heinrich A. 1962. "Ironie und Pathos in Raabes Novelle 'St. Thomas.'" 200-10.

Weniger, Erich. 1951. "Wilhelm Raabe und das bürgerliche Leben." 74-97.

Helmers, Hermann. 1968b. *Wilhelm Raabe.* Sammlung Metzler 71. Stuttgart: Metzler.

Klein, Johannes. 1968. "Raabes 'Schüdderump.'" *RJ.* 7-22.

Martini, Fritz. 1968. "Parodie und Regeneration der Idylle. Zu Wilhelm Raabes 'Horacker.'" *Literatur und Literaturgeschichte: Festgabe für Heinz Otto Burger*, ed. Reinhold Grimm and Conrad Wiedemann. Berlin: Erich Schmidt Verlag. 232-66.

Meyer, Herman. 1968. "Wilhelm Raabe. *Hastenbeck.*" Meyer, *The Poetics of Quotation in the European Novel*, tr. Theodore and Yetta Ziolkowski. Princeton: Princeton University Press. 204-29.

Ohl, Hubert. 1968. *Bild und Wirklichkeit: Studien zur Romankunst Raabes und Fontanes.* Heidelberg: Stiehm.

Sander, Volkmar. 1968. "Illusionszerstörung und Wirklichkeitserfassung im Roman Raabes."*Deutsche Romantheorien: Beiträge zu einer historischen Poetik des Romans in Deutschland*, ed. Reinhold Grimm. Frankfurt am Main and Bonn: Athenäum. 218-33.

Stankiewicz, Marketa. 1968. "The Tailor and the Sweeper: A New Look at Wilhelm Raabe." *Essays on German Literature in Honour of G. Joyce Hallamore*, ed. Michael S. Batts and Marketa Goetz Stankiewicz. Toronto: University of Toronto Press. 152-76.

Dietze, Walter. 1969. "Zeitstimmung und Zeitkritik in Wilhelm Raabes 'Chronik der Sperlingsgasse.'" *Monatshefte* 61: 337-46.

Goetz-Stankiewicz, Marketa. 1969. "Die böse Maske Moses Freudensteins. Gedanken zum Hungerpastor." *RJ.* 7-32.

Höhler, Gertrud. 1969. *Unruhige Gäste. Das Bibelzitat in Wilhelm Raabes Roman.* Bonn: Bouvier.

Klieneberger, H. R. 1969. "Charles Dickens and Wilhelm Raabe." *Oxford German Studies* 4: 90-117. Reprinted Klieneberger 1981.

The Novel in England and Germany: A Comparative Study. London: Oswald Wolff. 108-44.

Klopfenstein, Eduard. 1969. *Erzähler und Leser bei Wilhelm Raabe: Untersuchungen zu einem Formelement der Prosaerzählung.* Bern: Paul Haupt.

Martini, Fritz. 1969. "Wilhelm Raabe." *Deutsche Dichter des 19. Jahrhunderts,* ed. Benno von Wiese. Berlin: Erich Schmidt Verlag. 528-56.

Peterson, William S. 1969. *Interrogating the Oracle: A History of the London Browning Society.* Athens: Ohio University Press.

Radcliffe, Stanley. 1969. "Wilhelm Raabe, der Dreißigjährige Krieg und die Novelle." *RJ* . 57-70.

Bänsch, Dorothea. 1970. "Die Bibliothek Raabes. Nach Sachgebieten geordnet." *RJ.* 87-165.

David, Claude. 1970. "Über Wilhelm Raabes *Stopfkuchen.*" *Lebendige Form: Interpretationen zur deutschen Literatur. Festschrift für Heinrich E. K. Henel,* ed. Jeffrey L. Sammons and Ernst Schürer. Munich: Fink. 259-76.

Detroy, Peter. 1970. *Wilhelm Raabe: Der Humor als Gestaltungsprinzip im "Stopfkuchen."* Bonn: Bouvier.

Hotz, Karl. 1970. *Bedeutung und Funktion des Raumes im Werk Wilhelm Raabes.* Göppingen: Kümmerle.

Oppermann, Hans. 1970. *Raabe.* rororo Bildmonographie, 165. Reinbek bei Hamburg: Rowohlt.

Radcliffe, Stanley. 1970. "The Figure of the Eccentric in the Work of Wilhelm Raabe and its Significance for his Literary Achievement." Diss. University of Bristol.

Ringel, Karl Jürgen. 1970. *Wilhelm Raabes Roman "Hastenbeck." Ein Beitrag zum Verständnis des Alterswerkes.* Bern: Herbert Lang.

Delius, F. C. 1971. *Der Held und sein Wetter: Ein Kunstmittel und sein ideologischer Gebrauch im Roman des bürgerlichen Realismus.* Munich: Hanser.

Opie, Gerald. 1971. "Childhood and the Childlike in the Fiction of Wilhelm Raabe." Diss. University of Exeter.

Goetz-Stankiewicz, Marketa. 1972. "Der Schneider und der Feger. Zwei Grundgestalten bei Wilhelm Raabe." *RJ.* 31-60.

Hahn, Walter L. 1972. "Zum Erzählvorgang in Raabes 'Akten des Vogelsangs.'" *RJ.* 61-71.

O'Flaherty, James C., and Janet K. King, eds. 1972. Wilhelm Raabe, *Else von der Tanne with Translation and Commentary and an Introduction to Raabe's Life and Work.* University, Alabama: University of Alabama Press.

Angel, Pierre. 1973. *Le Personnage juif dans le roman allemand (1855-1915): La racine littéraire de l'antisémitisme Outre-Rhin.* Paris: Didier.

Dierkes, Hans. 1973. "Der 'Zauber des Gegensatzes.' Schopenhauer und Wilhelm Raabes 'Stopfkuchen.'" *Schopenhauer-Jahrbuch* 54: 93-107.

Ritterson, Michael Lee. 1973. "Narrators and Narration in Six Later Novels of Wilhelm Raabe." Diss. Harvard University.

Töteberg, M., and J. Zander. 1973. "Die Rezeption Raabes durch die 'Gesellschaft der Freunde Wilhelm Raabes' 1911 bis 1945." *RJ.* 178-93.

Clyde, Monica D. 1974. "Stopfkuchen: Raabe's Idyllic Sloth." *Pacific Coast Philology* 9: 25-30.

Kaiser, Katherine Starr. 1974. "Structure and Narrative Technique in Wilhelm Raabe's *Krähenfelder Geschichten.*" Diss. Brown University.

Meyen, Fritz. 1974. "Einige Bemerkungen zu Töteberg/Zander: 'Die Rezeption Raabes durch die 'Gesellschaft der Freunde Wilhelm Raabes' 1911 bis 1945 im 'Jahrbuch der Raabe-Gesellschaft' 1973, Seite 178-193." *RJ.* 105-11.

Radcliffe, S[tanley]. 1974. "Wilhelm Raabe and the Railway." *New German Studies* 2: 131-44.

Schweckendiek, Adolf. 1974. "Wilhelm Raabes 'Stopfkuchen': Eine ketzerische Betrachtung." *RJ.* 75-97.

Böttger, Fritz, ed. 1975. Wilhelm Raabe, *Die Gänse von Bützow.* Berlin: Verlag der Nation.

Matschke, Günter. 1975. *Die Isolation als Mittel der Gesellschaftskritik bei Wilhelm Raabe.* Bonn: Bouvier.

Reece, James Robert. 1975. "Narrator and Narrative Levels in Wilhelm Raabe's Stuttgart Novels." Diss. University of Oregon.

Steinecke, Hartmut. 1975. *Romantheorie und Romankritik in Deutschland: Die Entwicklung des Gattungsverständnisses von der Scott-Rezeption bis zum programmatischen Realismus.* Stuttgart: Metzler.

Bullivant, Keith. 1976. "Raabe and the European Novel." *Orbis Litterarum* 31: 263-81.

Derks, Paul. 1976. *Raabe-Studien: Beiträge zur Anwendung psychoanalytischer Interpretationsmodelle. Stopfkuchen und Das Odfeld.* Bonn: Bouvier.

Folkers, Gernot. 1976. *Besitz und Sicherheit: Über Entstehung und Zerfall einer bürgerlichen Illusion am Beispiel Goethes und Raabes.* Kronberg: Scriptor.

Gould, Stephan A. 1976. "Ontology and Ethics: The Rhetorical Role of the Narrator in Wilhelm Raabe's Early Novels." Diss. University of Nebraska.

Ritterson, Michael. 1976. "Rückwendung, Vorausdeutung und Erzählablauf in Wilhelm Raabes 'Das Odfeld' und 'Hastenbeck.'" *RJ.* 107-32.

Thürmer, Wilfried. 1976. "Entfremdetes Behagen. Wilhelm Raabes Erzählung 'Zum wilden Mann' als Konkretion gründerzeitlichen Bewußtseins." *RJ.* 151-61.

Webster, William T. 1976. See Webster 1982.

Koll, Rolf-Dieter. 1977. *Raumgestaltung bei Wilhelm Raabe.* Bonn: Bouvier.

Lensing, Leo A. 1977. *Narrative Structure and the Reader in Wilhelm Raabe's* Im alten Eisen. Berne, Frankfurt am Main, and Las Vegas: Peter Lang.

Mohr, Rudolf. 1977. "'Der Hungerpastor' — ein Pfarrerroman?" *RJ*. 48-85.

Rüter, Eugen. 1977. *Die Gesellschaft der Freunde Wilhelm Raabes: Rezeptionssteuerung als Programm*. Darmstadt: Thesen Verlag.

Sammons, Jeffrey L. 1977. *Literary Sociology and Practical Criticism: An Inquiry*. Bloomington: Indiana University Press.

Schrader, Hans-Jürgen. 1977. [Review of Rüter 1977.] *RJ*. 166-83.

Graves, Robert Anthony. 1978. "The Integral Personality: The Relationship between the Female Characters and the World in Selected Works of Theodor Fontane and Wilhelm Raabe." Diss. University of Bristol.

Kafitz, Dieter. 1978. *Figurenkonstellation als Mittel der Wirklichkeitserfassung. Dargestellt an Romanen der zweiten Hälfte des 19. Jahrhunderts: Freytag, Spielhagen, Fontane, Raabe*. Kronberg: Athenäum.

Radcliffe, Stanley. 1978. "Wilhelm Raabe und der Dreierklub zu Braunschweig." *RJ*. 11-16.

Schweikert, Rudi. 1978. "'Vom Hunger will ich handeln.' Überlegungen zur 'Hunger'-Metapher und zum Licht-Dunkel-Gegensatz in Wilhelm Raabes Roman 'Der Hungerpastor.'" *RJ*. 78-106.

Webster, William T. 1978. "Idealisierung oder Ironie? Verstehen und Mißverstehen in Wilhelm Raabes 'Stopfkuchen.'" *RJ*. 146-70.

Bachmann, Doris. 1979. "Die 'Dritte Welt' der Literatur. Eine ethnologische Methodenkritik literaturwissenschaftlichen Interpretierens, am Beispiel von Raabes Roman 'Abu Telfan oder Die Heimkehr vom Mondgebirge.'" *RJ*. 27-71.

Daemmrich, H. 1979. "Situationsanpassung als Daseinsgestaltung bei Raabe und Fontane." *Formen realistischer Erzählkunst: Festschrift for Charlotte Jolles. In Honour of her 70th Birthday*, ed. Jörg Thunecke and Eda Sagarra. Nottingham: Sherwood Press. 244-51.

Eason, Laurel Ellen. 1979. "Beginning and Conclusion: Structure and Theme in the Early Novels of Wilhelm Raabe." Diss. Vanderbilt University.

Eisele, Ulf. 1979. *Der Dichter und sein Detektiv: Raabes 'Stopfkuchen' und die Frage des Realismus.* Tübingen: Niemeyer.

Gelber, Mark. 1979. "Teaching 'Literary Anti-Semitism': Dickens' *Oliver Twist* and Freytag's *Soll und Haben.*" *Comparative Literature Studies* 16: 1-11.

Göhmann, Herbert W., and Matthias Göhmann. 1979. *Wilhelm Raabe und das Weserbergland: Ein Führer zu den Orten und Werken seiner Weserheimat.* Holzminden: Hüpke & Sohn, Weserland-Verlag.

Radcliffe, S[tanley]. 1979. "Historical Realities in Raabes *Im Siegeskranze.*" *Formen realistischer Erzählkunst: Festschrift for Charlotte Jolles. In Honour of her 70th Birthday,* ed. Jörg Thunecke and Eda Sagarra. Nottingham: Sherwood Press. 209-15.

Schultz, Hartwig. 1979. "Werk- und Autorintention in Raabes 'Alten Nestern' und 'Akten des Vogelsangs.'" *RJ.* 132-54.

Webster, W[illiam]. T. 1979a. "Hesitation and Decision: Wilhelm Raabe's Road to Reality." *Forum for Modern Language Studies* 15: 69-85.

_____. 1979b. "Social Change and Personal Insecurity in the Late Novels of Wilhelm Raabe."*Formen realistischer Erzählkunst: Festschrift for Charlotte Jolles. In Honour of her 70th Birthday,* ed. Jörg Thunecke and Eda Sagarra. Nottingham: Sherwood Press. 233-43.

Arendt, Dieter. 1980a. "Die Heine-Rezeption im Werk Wilhelm Raabes." *Heine-Jahrbuch* 19: 188-221.

_____. 1980b. "'Nun auf die Juden!' Figurationen des Judentums im Werk Wilhelm Raabes." *Tribüne* 19 (74): 108-40.

_____. 1980c. "Wilhelm Raabes Dramaturgie der Erzählkunst." *RJ.* 7-42.

Denkler, Horst. 1980a. "Wilhelm Raabe: Pfisters Mühle (1884). Zur Aktualität eines alten Themas und vom Nutzen offener Strukturen." *Romane und Erzählungen des Bürgerlichen Realismus: Neue Interpretationen,* ed. Horst Denkler. Stuttgart: Reclam. 293-309.

_____, ed. 1980b. Wilhelm Raabe, *Pfisters Mühle: Ein Sommerferienheft.* Stuttgart: Reclam.

Fries, Marilyn Sibley. 1980. *The Changing Consciousness of Reality: The Image of Berlin in Selected German Novels from Raabe to Döblin.* Bonn: Bouvier.

Goedsche, Charlotte L. 1980. See Goedsche 1989.

Heldt, Uwe. 1980. *Isolation and Identität: Die Bedeutung des Idyllischen in der Epik Wilhelm Raabes.* Frankfurt am Main, Bern, and Cirencester: Peter D. Lang.

Mayer, Gerhart. 1980. "Wilhelm Raabe und die Tradition des Bildungsromans." *RJ.* 97-124.

Mayer, Hans. 1980. "Wilhelm Raabe. *Abu Telfan oder die Heimkehr vom Mondgebirge." Die Zeit.* July 19. 39. Expanded 1980 in *ZEIT-Bibliothek der 100 Bücher,* ed. Fritz J. Raddatz. Frankfurt am Main: Suhrkamp. 278-82. Reprinted Lensing/Peter 1981. 128-32.

Schedlinsky, Walter. 1980. *Rolle und industriegesellschaftliche Entwicklung: Die literarische Vergegenständlichung eines sozialgeschichtlichen Phänomens im Werk Wilhelm Raabes.* Frankfurt am Main: R. G. Fischer.

Webster, William T. 1980. "Thomas Mann, Wilhelm Raabe und die realistische Tradition in Deutschland." *Zeitschrift für deutsche Philologie* 99: 254-76.

Bröhan, Margrit. 1981. *Die Darstellung der Frau bei Wilhelm Raabe und ein Vergleich mit liberalen Positionen zur Emanzipation der Frau im 19. Jahrhundert.* Frankfurt am Main and Bern: Peter D. Lang.

Daemmrich, Horst S. 1981. *Wilhelm Raabe.* Twayne's World Authors Series, 594. Boston: Twayne.

Daum, J., and Wolf-D. Schuegraf. 1981. *Verzeichnis der Bestände von und über Wilhelm Raabe in Braunschweig.* Braunschweig: Stadtarchiv.

Di Maio, Irene Stocksieker. 1981a. *The Multiple Perspective: Wilhelm Raabe's Third-Person Narratives of the Braunschweig Period.* Amsterdam: Benjamins.

Klieneberger, H. R. 1981. See Klieneberger 1969.

Kolbe, Hans. 1981a. *Wilhelm Raabe: Vom Entwicklungs- zum Desillusionierungsroman.* Berlin: Akademie Verlag.

Lensing, Leo A., and Hans-Werner Peter, eds. 1981. *Wilhelm Raabe: Studien zu seinem Leben und Werk.* Braunschweig: pp-Verlag.
Includes:
Denkler, Horst. 1981. "Die Antwort literarischer Phantasie auf eine der 'größeren Fragen der Zeit.' Zu Wilhelm Raabes Erzähltext *Pfisters Mühle.*" 234-54. Reprinted Denkler 1988a, 81-102.
Di Maio, Irene Stocksieker. 1981b. "The 'Frauenfrage' and the Reception of Wilhelm Raabe's Female Characters." 406-13.
Geisler, Eberhard. 1981. "Abschied vom Herzensmuseum. Die Auflösung des Poetischen Realismus in Wilhelm Raabes *Akten des Vogelsangs.*" 365-80.
Hanson, William P. 1981. "New Realities: Common Concerns in Raabe and Hardy." 255-65.
Kolbe, Hans. 1981b. "Das Exzeptionelle bei Wilhelm Raabe." 504-20.
Lensing, Leo A. 1981b. "A Report on Raabe Scholarship in the United States. Dissertations and Books 1950-1981." 521-39.
Opie, Gerald. 1981. "Raabe and the Classical Tradition: Some Reflections on *Der Dräumling.*" 133-50.
Radcliffe, Stanley. 1981. "Historische Wirklichkeit in Wilhelm Raabes *Im Siegeskranze.*" 115-27.
Sammons, Jeffrey L. 1981. "Wilhelm Raabes *Stopfkuchen.* Pro and Contra." 281-98.
Sengle, Friedrich. 1981. "*Der Hungerpastor* (1863/64): Zum Problem der frühen Biedermeiertradition." 77-98.

Webster, William T. 1981. "Psychiatrische Beobachtungen oder Gesellschaftskritik? Zur Darstellung geistiger Abnormalitäten im Werk Wilhelm Raabes." 324-41.

Martini, Fritz. 1981. "Wilhelm Raabes Verzicht auf 'Versöhnung.' Bemerkungen zu 'Meister Autor.'" *RJ*. 169-93.

Meyer, Eberhard W. 1981. "Raabe — mit Vergnügen." *Diskussion Deutsch* No. 57: 3-5.

Meyer, Jochen. 1981. *Wilhelm Raabe: Unter Demokraten, Hoflieferanten und Philistern. Eine Chronik seiner Stuttgarter Jahre.* Stuttgart: Fleischhauer & Spohn.

Peter, Hans-Werner, ed. 1981. Wilhelm Raabe, *Werke in Auswahl: Studienausgabe.* 9 volumes. Braunschweig: pp-Verlag.

Preisendanz, Wolfgang. 1981. "Die Erzählstruktur als Bedeutungskomplex der 'Akten des Vogelsangs.'" *RJ*. 210-24.

Sander, Volkmar. 1981. "Corviana non leguntur. Gedanken zur Raabe-Rezeption in Amerika und England." *RJ*. 118-27.

Sporn, Thomas. 1981. "Wilhelm Raabe: Ökologisch?" *Diskussion Deutsch* No. 57: 56-63.

Emrich, Wilhelm. 1982. "Persönlichkeit und Zivilisation in Wilhelm Raabes 'Die Akten des Vogelsangs.'" *RJ*. 7-25.

Hajek, Siegfried, and Fritz Martini. 1982. "Diskussionshorizonte: 'Meister Autor' im Kontext realistischen Erzählens." *RJ*. 99-109.

Radcliffe, S[tanley]. 1982a. "The Diary of a Somebody? Wilhelm Raabe's Record of his Life." *New German Studies* 10: 107-22.

_____. 1982b. "Raabe, Jensens 'Altes Wort' und 'The Quarterly Review.'" *RJ*. 142-47.

Webster, William T. 1982a. "Der 'Hinhocker' und der 'Weltwanderer': Zur Bedeutung der Reise bei Wilhelm Raabe." *RJ*. 26-39.

_____. 1982b. *Wirklichkeit und Illusion in den Romanen Wilhelm Raabes.* Raabe-Forschungen, ed. H.-W. Peter, 1. Braunschweig: pp-Verlag.

Brewster, Philip J[ames]. 1983a. "Onkel Ketschwayo in Neuteuto-
burg. Zeitgeschichtliche Anspielungen in Raabes 'S-
topfkuchen.'" *RJ*. 96-118.

_____. "Wilhelm Raabes historische Fiktion im Kontext:
Beitrag zur Rekonstruktion der Gattungsproblematik zwischen
Geschichtsschreibung und Poesie im 19. Jahrhundert." Diss.
Cornell University.

Hanson, William P. 1983. "Raabes erste Chronik." *RJ*. 33-48.

Lensing, Leo A. 1983. "Reading Raabe: The Example of Kurt
Tucholsky." *Seminar* 19: 122-35.

Peter, Hans-Werner. 1983. *Wilhelm Raabe: Der Dichter in seinen
Federzeichnungen und Skizzen*. Rosenheim: Rosenheimer
Verlagshaus.

Sander, Volkmar, ed. 1983. Wilhelm Raabe, *Novels*. Foreword by
Joel Agee. The German Library, Vol. 45. New York: Continuum.

Bullivant, Keith. 1984. "Realismus und Romanästhetik: Überlegungen zu einem problematischen Aspekt der deutschen
Literatur." *Orbis Litterarum* 39: 1-13.

Denkler, Horst. 1984. "Wohltäter Maienborn. Ängste und ihre
Bewältigung im Werk Wilhelm Raabes." *RJ*. 7-25. Reprinted
Denkler 1988a, 48-65.

Dittrich, Wolfgang. 1984. "Hans Butzmann † und sein Beitrag zur
Raabe-Philologie. Mit einer unpublizierten Studie (1957) zu
editorischen Fragen der 'Braunschsweiger Ausgabe.'" *RJ*. 51-67.

Holub, Robert C. *Reception Theory: A Critical Introduction*. London and New York: Methuen.

Kaiser, Nancy A. "Reading Raabe's Realism: *Die Akten des Vogelsangs*." *Germanic Review* 59: 2-9.

Klingenberg, Anneliese, ed. 1984. Wilhelm Raabe, *Der Dräumling*.
Mit Dokumenten zur Schillerfeier 1859. Berlin and Weimar:
Aufbau.

Noltenius, Rainer. 1984. *Dichterfeiern in Deutschland: Rezep-
tionsgeschichte als Sozialgeschichte am Beispiel der Schiller-
und Freiligrath-Feiern*. Munich: Fink.

Radcliffe, Stanley. 1984. *Der Sonderling im Werk Wilhelm Raabes.* Raabe-Forschungen, ed. Hans-Werner Peter, 2. Braunschweig: pp-Verlag.

Zwilgmeyer, Franz. 1984. "Archetypische Bewußtseinsstufen in Raabes Werken, insbesondere in den 'Akten des Vogelsangs.'" *RJ.* 99-120.

Denkler, Horst. 1985. "Der untrügliche Spürsinn des Genius für seinesgleichen. Arno Schmidts Verhältnis zu Wilhelm Raabe." *RJ.* 138-53. Reprinted Denkler 1988a, 123-38.

Garzmann, Manfred R. W., and Wolf-Dieter Schuegraf, eds. 1985. *Raabe-Verzeichnis: Bestände in Braunschweig Marbach/ Neckar und Wolfenbüttel.* Braunschweig: Stadtarchiv und Städtische Bibliotheken.

Hanson, William P. 1985a. "Komik und Elend in Raabes Erzählung 'Der Marsch nach Hause.'" *RJ.* 48-62.

_____. 1985b. "Raabe's Poems." *Modern Language Review.* 80: 858-70.

Horch, Hans Otto. 1985. "Judenbilder in der realistischen Erzählliteratur. Jüdische Figuren bei Gustav Freytag, Fritz Reuter, Berthold Auerbach und Wilhelm Raabe." *Juden und Judentum in der Literatur*, ed. Herbert A. Strauss and Christhard Hoffmann. Munich: Deutscher Taschenbuchverlag. 140-71.

Sammons, Jeffrey L. 1985a. "The Mill on the Sewer: Wilhelm Raabe's *Pfister's Mill* and the Present Relevance of Past Literature." *Orbis Litterarum* 40: 16-32.

_____. 1985b. "Raabe's Ravens." *Michigan German Studies* 9: 1-15.

Schrader, Hans-Jürgen, ed. 1985. Wilhelm Raabe, *Werke in Einzelausgaben.* 10 volumes. Frankfurt am Main: Insel.

Denkler, Horst. 1986a. "Marie Jensen. Angaben zur Person einer schönen Unbekannten." *Mitt.* 73: 5-8. Reprinted Denkler 1988a, 43-47.

_____. 1986b. "Zugewanderter, Bürger, Ehrenbürger. Braunschweig im Leben Wilhelm Raabes." *RJ.* 35-44. Reprinted Denkler 1988a, 32-40.

Hanson, William. 1986. "Raabe's Region." *Seminar* 22: 277-98.

Hoffmann, Volker. 1986. "'Zum wilden Mann.' Die anthropologische und poetologische Reduktion des Teufelspaktthemas in der Literatur des Realismus am Beispiel von Wilhelm Raabes Erzählung." *Jahrbuch der Deutschen Schillergesellschaft* 30: 472-92.

Meyer-Krentler, Eckhardt. 1986a. "Homerisches und wirkliches Blau. Wilhelm Raabe und sein Wetter." *RJ*. 50-82.

_____. 1986b. *"Unterm Strich": Literarischer Markt, Trivialität und Romankunst in Raabes "Der Lar."* Paderborn, Munich, Vienna, and Zurich: Schöningh.

Sammons, Jeffrey L. 1986. "Wilhelm Raabe and his Reputation Among Jews and Anti-Semites." *Identity and Ethos: A Festschrift for Sol Liptzin on the Occasion of his 85th Birthday,* ed. Mark H. Gelber. New York, Berne, and Frankfurt am Main: Peter Lang. 169-91.

Zirbs, Wieland. 1986. *Strukturen des Erzählens: Studien zum Spätwerk Wilhelm Raabes.* Frankfurt am Main, Bern, and New York: Peter Lang.

Denkler, Horst. 1987a. "Panier aufwerfen für Raabe. Zur Geschichte der 'Raabe-Pflege' im Bannkreis der Raabe-Gesellschaft." *RJ*. 11-23. Reprinted Denkler 1988a, 139-52.

_____. 1987b. "Das 'wirckliche Juda' und der 'Renegat': Moses Freudenstein als Kronzeuge für Wilhelm Raabes Verhältnis zu Juden und Judentum." *German Quarterly* 60: 5-18. Reprinted Denkler 1988a, 66-80.

Di Maio, Irene S. 1987. "Nochmals zu den 'Akten': Sphinx, Indianerprinzessin, Nilschlange." *RJ*. 228-42.

Holub, Robert C. 1987. "Raabe's Impartiality: A Reply to Horst Denkler." *German Quarterly* 60: 617-22.

Meyer-Krentler, Eckhardt. 1987. "Stopfkuchen — Ein Doppelgänger. Wilhelm Raabe erzählt Theodore Storm." *RJ*. 179-204.

Royer, Jean. 1987. "Leonie des Beaux und ihr Lied: von Südfrankreich nach Berlin." *RJ*. 243-55.

Sammons, Jeffrey L. 1987. *Wilhelm Raabe: The Fiction of the Alternative Community*. Princeton: Princeton University Press.

Thunecke, Jörg. 1987. "'Such a firm earth and such an ethereal sky.' Die Thematisierung assimilatorischer und zionistischer Tendenzen in Wilhelm Raabes 'Hungerpastor' und George Eliots 'Daniel Deronda.'" *RJ*. 156-78.

Arndt, Karl. 1988. "Der zeichnende Wilhelm Raabe. Anmerkungen und Beobachtungen zu Stil und Herkunft seiner Kunst." *RJ*. 110-44.

Denkler, Horst. 1988a. *Neues über Wilhelm Raabe: Zehn Annäherungsversuche an einen verkannten Schriftsteller*. Tübingen: Niemeyer.

_____. 1988b. "'In *Berlin* nicht zu ermitteln': Berlin im Leben Wilhelm Raabes." *RJ*. 9-23. Reprinted Denkler 1988a, 17-31.

Goldammer, Peter. 1988. "''Kritisch' oder 'historisch-kritisch'? Reflexionen über eine neu zu schaffende Raabe-Ausgabe." *RJ*. 39-51.

Hohendahl, Peter Uwe, ed. 1988. *A History of German Literary Criticism, 1730-1980*. Lincoln and London: University of Nebraska Press.

Lensing, Leo A. 1988. "Naturalismus, Religion und Sexualität. Zur Frage der Auseinandersetzung mit Zola in Wilhelm Raabes 'Unruhige Gäste.'" *RJ*. 145-67.

Meyer, Jochen. 1988. *Albert Dulk, ein Achtundvierziger: Aus dem Lebensroman eines Radikalen*. Marbacher Magazin, 48. Marbach am Neckar: Deutsche Schillergesellschaft.

Mikoletzky, Juliane. 1988. *Die deutsche Amerika-Auswanderung des 19. Jahrhunderts in der zeitgenössischen fiktionalen Literatur*. Tübingen: Niemeyer.

Nägele, Rainer. 1988. "Kein Schlußstrich: Thinking the Unthought (A Postscript to Horst Denkler's Non-Response)." *German Quarterly* 61: 284-86.

Richter, Helmut. 1988. "Wilhelm Raabe und das Junge Deutschland. Ein Diskussionbeitrag zum literarischen Standort des
Dichters." *RJ*. 76-109.

Roebling, Irmgard. 1988. *Wilhelm Raabes doppelte Buchführung:
Paradigma einer Spaltung.* Tübingen: Niemeyer.

Rohse, Eberhard. 1988. "'Transcendentale Menschenkunde' im
Zeichen des Affen. Raabes literarische Antworten auf die Dar-
winismusdebatte des 19. Jahrhunderts." *RJ*. 168-210.

Sammons, Jeffrey L. 1988. *Raabe: Pfisters Mühle.* Critical Guides to
German Texts, ed. Martin Swales, No. 9. London: Grant &
Cutler.

Brenner, Peter J. 1989. "Die Einheit der Welt. Zur Entzauberung der
Fremde und Verfremdung der Heimat in Raabes 'Abu Telfan.'"
RJ. 45-62.

Denkler, Horst. 1989a. "Verantwortungsethik. Zu Wilhelm Raabes
Umgang mit Juden und Judentum." *Conditio Judaica: Juden-
tum, Antisemitismus und deutschsprachige Literatur vom 18.
Jahrhundert bis zum Ersten Weltkrieg,* ed. Hans Otto Horch and
Horst Denkler, Vol. 2. Tübingen: Niemeyer. 148-68.

_____. 1989b. *Wilhelm Raabe: Legende — Leben —
Literatur.* Tübingen: Niemeyer.

Goedsche, Charlotte L. 1989. *Narrative Structures in Wilhelm
Raabe's* Die Chronik der Sperlingsgasse. New York, Bern,
Frankfurt am Main, and Paris: Peter Lang.

Lehrer, Mark. 1989,. "Der ausgegrabene Heinrich Schliemann und
der begrabene Theodor Storm. Anspielungen auf Zeitgenossen
in Raabes 'Stopfkuchen.'" *RJ*. 63-90.

Sammons, Jeffrey L., ed. 1989. Wilhelm Raabe, "Celtic Bones"; "St.
Thomas." *German Novellas of Realism II.* The German Library,
Vol. 39. New York: Continuum. 29-108.

Schrader, Hans-Jürgen. 1989. "Gedichtete Dichtungstheorie im
Werk Raabes. Exemplifiziert an 'Alte Nester.'" *RJ*. 1-27.

Detering, Heinrich. 1990. *Theodizee und Erzählverfahren: Narrative Experimente mit religiösen Modellen im Werk Wilhelm Raabes*. Göttingen: Vandenhoeck & Ruprecht.

Index

DATE DUE

NOV 06 2006		

WITHDRAWN